why do we suffer?

why do we suffer?

a scriptural approach
to the human condition

Daniel J. Harrington, S.J.

A SHEED & WARD BOOK

ROWMAN & LITTLEFIELD PUBLISHERS, INC.
Lanham • Boulder • New York • Toronto • Plymouth, UK

Published by Sheed & Ward
An imprint of Rowman & Littlefield Publishers, Inc.
A wholly owned subsidary of The Rowman & Littlefield Publishing Group, Inc.
4501 Forbes Boulevard, Suite 200
Lanham, MD 20706

Estover Road
Plymouth PL6 7PY
United Kingdom

Distributed by National Book Network

Cover photograph © Burton Pritzker/Photonica
Cover design by Kathy Kikkert
Interior design by GrafixStudio, Inc.

Scripture quotations are taken from *The New Revised Standard Version* of the Bible, ©
1989 by the Division of Christian Education of the National Council of the Churches of
Christ in the USA. Used by permission. All rights reserved.

Library of Congress Cataloging-in-Publication Data

Harrington, Daniel, J.
    Why do we suffer? : a scriptural approach to the human condition / Daniel J.
Harrington
        p. cm.
    ISBN 1-58051-043-4 (pbk. : alk. paper)
        1. Suffering—Biblical teaching. I. Title.
    BS680.S.854 H37 2000
    231'.8—dc21   99-057646
                                                            CIP
Printed in the United States of America.

⊖™ The paper used in this publication meets the minimum requirements of
American National Standard for Information Sciences—Permanence of
Paper for Printed Library Materials, ANSI/NISO Z39.48-1992.

Contents

❧

Prologue:

Suffering and the Bible

∽

S UFFERING is part of human existence; we all know that. Everyone suffers in some way at some time; we all know that. And yet, when suffering visits us personally, we feel isolated and abandoned ("poor me!"). We all know people who tell us, "I cannot believe in a God who would allow such suffering." Perhaps we ourselves have said this or at least thought it. Suffering is part of human existence. And yet, suffering remains threatening, challenging, and mysterious.

Throughout the centuries many suffering people have found consolation and direction in sacred Scripture. Others have been "turned off" by the Bible's link between sin and suffering and by its emphasis on sacrifice and redemptive suffering. In fact, the Bible presents not one but many approaches to suffering. This book explains the Bible's various approaches to suffering with reference to key texts. It gives particular attention to Old Testament passages, since the Old Testament deals extensively with suffering and provides the vocabulary, concepts, and context for much of what the New Testament says about suffering.

Besides being a survey of biblical approaches to suffering, this book also takes the problem of suffering as a way of introducing large parts of the Bible to a nonspecialist audience. The Bible is a collection of books from various times and places, and many readers find it hard to get a handle on it. One theme that runs through the various books of the Bible is suffering—a theme that naturally evokes questions about the existence and nature of God, the human condition, ethics, justice, evil, sin, rewards and punishments, and life after death. By using suffering as a point of entry to the Bible, I hope that readers will be better able to connect the Scriptures to their own experiences and at the same time be more confident and eager to read these books for the many other wonderful things in them.

So this book seeks to be both a survey of biblical approaches to suffering and a general introduction to many parts of the Bible. It uses suffering as a lens. As a Catholic, I include in my canon the so-called Old Testament Apocrypha or Deuterocanonical books. These late biblical books are especially rich resources in dealing with the theme of suffering and related issues.

I write as a Christian, a Jesuit priest, and a biblical scholar. I am convinced that the Old Testament constitutes an essential source for Christian theology. For me, Jesus and the New Testament writings are unintelligible apart from what we call the Old Testament. I am also convinced that what the Bible says about suffering can and does speak to people in the twenty-first century. And so, after each exposition of a biblical approach to suffering, I offer reflections on what the approach might say positively ("Possibilities") to suffering people today, and what cautions ("Problems") need to be taken into account. The goal of the section titled "Questions for Reflection, Discussion, and Prayer" that concludes each chapter is to facilitate the reader's personal assimilation of the biblical material. I include a basic bibliography of books ("For Further Study") that approach the mystery of suffering from the perspectives of the Bible and theology. The theological studies generally take the Bible as their starting point but move into important areas not covered in the Bible.

Despite its many positive accomplishments, the twentieth century was a time of suffering on a massive scale, from the Armenian genocide to "ethnic cleansing" in the Balkans. Emblematic of twentieth-century suffering was the destruction of six million Jews in the 1940s. This event known as the *Shoah* ("destruction") or the *Holocaust* ("whole burnt offering") has proved both the value (laments, Job) and the inadequacy (the law of retribution) of the biblical approaches to suffering.

The destruction of the European Jewish community, surely one of the defining events of the twentieth century, has evoked many different interpretations and explanations from Jews and non-Jews alike. The famous scene of the public execution by hanging of a Jewish boy in Elie Wiesel's *Night* captures the horror and the challenge of the Shoah: "Behind me, I heard the same man asking: 'Where is God now?' And I heard a voice within me answer him: 'Where is He? Here He is—He is hanging here on this gallows.'" This poignant scene has been taken to mean that God is dead, that the Jewish people are dead, that God is really present in the suffering of the dying boy, that evil has triumphed over God, or that Jewish victimhood must end. Christians, of course, see the crucified Jesus in the boy's sufferings, although this was not Wiesel's intention.

The Shoah has raised many difficult theological questions: Where was God in all this? Are there limits to God's power and/or justice? Does God still enter into history? Is evil stronger than good in humans? Is human freedom a sufficient explanation? What about God's election of and providential care for Israel? Is there any proportion between Israel's alleged sins and this punishment? Can one really say that God brings good out of such a massive evil? Where does Jesus fit in all this?

Jews and Christians approach these questions in different ways. Although the Bible does not have all the answers, it does offer some resources to believers. The lament psalms of the Old Testament provide the vocabulary for sufferers and give them permission to express emotions and hold out hope. The fearless exploration of the problem of innocent suffering in the Book of Job warns against giving easy answers and cheap expressions of piety to suffering people. And the New Testament reminds us that Jesus was part of a long tradition of Jewish suffering.

One of the most striking documents that emerged from the Shoah was a short story by Zvi Kolitz entitled "Yossel Rakover's Appeal to God." This work of fiction first published in 1947 took as its setting the Warsaw Ghetto uprising in April 1943. It presents Yossel Rakover's "last words" as he faces certain death. In his meditation, in which he searches for answers regarding his own suffering and especially that of the Jewish people, Yossel often alludes to the various biblical approaches to suffering. As a way of bridging the gap between the world of the Bible and our own age, I preface each of the first five chapters with a brief quotation from "Yossel Rakover's Appeal to God." The remaining three chapters are introduced by appropriate New Testament texts.

I recognize that the Bible does not have all the answers about the mystery of suffering. Indeed some sincere religious people have confessed that none of the biblical approaches have "worked" in helping them to understand and cope with their own suffering. But many more bear witness to the comfort and orientation that the Bible has given them as they have confronted their own mystery of suffering.

With this book I want to help suffering people and those who care for them to recognize and appreciate the resources available in Scripture, and to use those resources intelligently and constructively. This is a book about a book. My aim is to illumine the biblical texts about suffering and to illustrate how to read the Bible through the lens of suffering. I suggest that my own comments be read alongside the Bible itself, and that they serve as a starting point for meditation, discussion, and prayer on the pertinent biblical passages. I have quoted from the New Revised Standard Version of the Bible, but the material in this book can be used with any modern Bible translation.

I became especially interested in this topic about twenty years ago in connection with my father's sudden death and my mother's various illnesses—and have taught courses on the topic in one form or another almost every year since. I claim no special gift of compassion or pastoral wisdom in dealing with suffering; indeed I am not good at facing the unpleasant realities of life or responding instinctively to the needs of others. Suffering presents as much a problem to me as it does to anyone, perhaps even more so. Yet I am convinced that familiarity with the various biblical approaches can make a positive contribution for those who suffer and for those who try to help and love them.

There is an old saying: "Those who can't do teach." I have often felt the truth of that statement as I answered questions during lectures, presided over discussions, and read my students' essays on the Bible and suffering. From their attempts to put their personal and pastoral experiences of suffering together with Scripture and theology, I have learned so much and have become a little better at "doing."

About the mystery of suffering, neither the Bible nor I have all the answers. I humbly present this little book as a small contribution to the conversation about the Bible and suffering. I dedicate it to the memory of a former student and good friend, Rev. Mark F. Toohey, S.J. (1958–1999) who, through ten years of living with a brain tumor, taught me much about courage and faith in the face of the mystery of suffering.

Chapter One

Coping with Suffering: The Lament Psalms

I believe in You, God of Israel, even though You have done everything to stop me from believing in You. . . . I bow my head before Your greatness, but will not kiss the lash with which You strike me.

—Yossel Rakover

TO SUFFER is to feel pain or distress; to sustain injury, disadvantage, or loss; or to undergo a penalty. Suffering can be physical, psychological, or spiritual, and it can take many forms. One can lose a loved one (a spouse, child, or friend) or property (by theft, fire, and so forth) or reputation (as a victim of slander). A common type of suffering is associated with sickness, whether from a chronic condition or a catastrophic event (a stroke). Being a victim of violence (by rape or assault) or of discrimination (because of ethnic identity, gender, physical disability, or social status) also counts as suffering. Or one can lose "everything" to hurricane, tornado, fire, or some other natural disaster. More subtle but very real forms of suffering result from failure to pass an exam, to get a position, or to achieve some other goal.

No one gets through life without some suffering. While some people seem to be "victim souls," others go through life apparently unscathed. But in the last analysis, suffering is a universal experience for human beings. And while we all know this, our suffering is frequently a very subjective (why me?) and isolating (we assume that no one else is suffering) experience. Although we all know the usual pieces of advice given to sufferers, most of us are dissatisfied with that advice, especially when it is applied to our own situation.

In our immediate and instinctual reaction to suffering, we may try to deny it, flee it, or resist it directly, or we may simply be immobilized by it. On the longer view, we may work hard to find the cause of the suffering, either to stop the suffering or at least to understand it (and thus gain a certain mastery over it). Some people respond to suffering by turning to religion, getting drunk, or going shopping. Some people take suffering as a message or a discipline, and use it as the occasion to reorient or redefine their lives and their worldviews.

The theological problem raised by the experience of suffering is generally called *theodicy*. Derived from the Greek words for "God" (*theos*) and "justice" (*dike*), theodicy refers to the attempt to hold together these three propositions: God is all powerful; God is just; and people suffer. To put it another way, how can an omnipotent and just God allow suffering (especially innocent suffering)? In answering this question, a believer seeks to "justify the ways of God" against the horizon of real suffering.

There are many approaches to suffering in the Bible. All of them are worth understanding and may be of help in dealing with our own suffering and that of others. Yet no one of these approaches is fully satisfactory when taken on its own. In this volume we will take the experience of suffering as a starting point, and explore how the biblical traditions deal with suffering. While encompassing both Testaments and giving special attention to the Old Testament because it is so foundational for the New Testament on the topic, this study takes as its framework the paschal mystery—Jesus' passion, death, and resurrection—as its theological framework. My hope is that readers may come to a greater appreciation of what Scripture says about suffering, and that they may grow in their personal, theological, and pastoral approaches to it.

The first approach in this book is suggested by the many songs about suffering in the Old Testament Book of Psalms. These are called *Laments*, and they illustrate how some people in ancient Israel coped with their suffering. The word "cope," however, may suggest too much passivity to convey what the lament psalms are about. In fact, these psalms are full of activity; the speaker addresses God directly and boldly. In some cases God is criticized as the cause of the suffering; in other cases God is reminded that God's own reputation and honor are at risk. These psalms include a surprising amount of complaining about suffering and frequent challenges for God to do something. We find few inhibitions or excuses about bringing up the subject of suffering in these psalms. Today, the lament psalms can help sufferers develop a vocabulary about their condition, raise the theological issues at stake in their suffering, and recognize that as human beings and religious people we belong to a community of fellow sufferers.

The Conventions of the Laments

Appreciation of the psalms has been greatly enriched by modern scholarly insights about their literary forms and original settings in the life of ancient Israel. The psalms often follow certain outlines or "scripts," and fall into a few literary categories: hymns of praise to God, psalms connected with the king and the royal household, wisdom psalms, prayers of supplication, and laments. The largest category by far is the lament: a statement about the sorry condition of an individual or the people, and a plea for divine help. Many of these psalms appear to have had some connection with the rituals of worship in the Jerusalem temple. Most of the laments end on a note of praise and thanks to God, thus suggesting that they were sung or recited in connection with the thanksgiving sacrifices offered at the temple.

The basic elements, or "script," for the lament psalms can be grasped easily by looking at Psalm 3. After an address to God ("O LORD"), there is a complaint (3:1–2): "How many are my foes! Many are rising against me; many are saying to me, 'There is no help for you in God.'" Although the precise nature of the psalmist's suffering is left vague, this vagueness allows the psalm to be used by more than one person. Indeed the "open" character of these psalms makes it possible for us to find meaning in them thousands of years after their original composition.

Psalm 3 is introduced by a heading or superscription: "A Psalm of David, when he fled from his son Absalom." The reference is to 2 Samuel 15:13–31—the sad scene of David and his household leaving Jerusalem because "the hearts of the Israelites have gone after Absalom" (15:13). Rather than taking this event as the historical occasion for the composition of Psalm 3, it is better to view the event as an actualization of the psalm. In other words, Psalm 3 expresses what David would or should have said as he left Jerusalem.

Following the complaint is the confession of trust in God (3:3–6). Here the psalmist acknowledges the Lord as "a shield around me, my glory, and the one who lifts up my head" (3:3). Whereas the opponents taunt him about there being "no help for you in God," the psalmist remains firm in trusting God. God has answered his prayers in the past "from his holy hill" (3:4), surely a reference to the Jerusalem temple on Mount Zion. The repeated human act of sleeping and waking he takes as proof of God's power and care (3:5). With God on his side, the psalmist claims, he is not "afraid of ten thousands of people who have set themselves against me all around" (3:6). This confession of faith expresses a confidence in God based on past experience.

The petition (3:7) asks God directly ("O LORD") to rise up and deliver the speaker. Part of his vindication involves the shaming of his (and God's) enemies. The imagery is violent:

"For you strike all my enemies on the cheek; you break the teeth of the wicked." Note that God, not the speaker, is presumed to be the agent of vengeance, and that these are more likely images rather than concrete expectations.

The concluding thanksgiving (3:8) affirms that "deliverance belongs to the LORD," perhaps suggesting that in this case (as in most lament psalms) the deliverance from suffering has already taken place and that the speaker is now offering a thanksgiving sacrifice. The final line ("may your blessing be on your people") places the psalm in the collective context of the experience of God's people.

Psalm 3 introduces us to the literary conventions of the biblical laments. It consists of an address to God and a complaint (3:1–2), a confession of confidence in God (3:3–6), a petition (3:7), and a concluding thanksgiving (3:8). The nature of the suffering is vague, thus facilitating the psalm's reuse by many people and serving something like a "greeting card" today. The speaker addresses God in a free, even bold manner, appealing to God to vindicate both him and the divine honor. And there are some hints at a connection with worship at the Jerusalem temple: "from his holy hill . . . Deliverance belongs to the LORD" (3:4, 8).

The basic elements of the biblical lament recur in Psalm 13 (and in almost every other lament), but the order here is different. After the address to God ("O LORD"), Psalm 13 places the complaint in verses 1–2, and the question, "How long?" is repeated four times. The content of the complaint is that God seems to have abandoned the speaker, with the result that the speaker suffers ("pain in my soul . . . sorrow in my heart") and his enemy seems to be winning out. While appropriate to David's experience ("A Psalm of David"), Psalm 13 can apply to many other persons. The petition (13:3–4), for example, asks for God's help ("Consider and answer me") and reminds God that failure to act will result in the psalmist's death ("I will sleep the sleep of death") and in his enemy's apparent vindication ("I have prevailed").

The confession and thanksgiving are woven together in 13:5–6. The tenses of the verbs ("I trusted . . . he has dealt bountifully with me") give the impression that the crisis has been resolved and that the psalm now serves as a thanksgiving. The resolution of the crisis is attributed to trust in God's "steadfast love"—a very important biblical concept. And the psalmist fully expects that in the future his heart "shall rejoice in your salvation."

The biblical laments like Psalms 3 and 13 can be of great aid for those who find themselves in the midst of suffering. On the psychological level, these psalms help sufferers get in touch with their intense emotions and address God directly and without religious censorship. On the social level, they encourage sufferers (who usually feel alone and misunderstood) to recognize that they belong to a tradition of suffering and a community of sufferers. We are not alone. On the theological level, they help sufferers face the reality of suffering and articulate their own questions: Why am I suffering? Where is God? Why isn't God doing something for me? Why are "they" allowed to triumph over me and God?

Psalm 22 and Jesus

According to Mark 15:34 and Matthew 27:46, Jesus' final words from the cross were "My God, my God, why have you forsaken me?" These words fascinate people today; they often wonder whether Jesus underwent some kind of final despair. In fact, these words are the opening of Psalm 22—a lament often described as the "psalm of the righteous sufferer." Only by looking at the whole psalm, including its ending in the speaker's vindication and thanksgiving, can we appreciate what the Evangelists were saying by reporting Psalm 22 as the final words of Jesus.

All the conventions of the lament psalms appear in Psalm 22, but in a more complex way than in Psalms 3 and 13. The first part (22:1–21a) mixes complaints and confessions of trust, and climaxes in a petition. The second part (22:21b–31) assumes a mood of vindication, thanksgiving, and celebration.

After the address ("My God, my God"), there is an alternation between complaints (22:1–2, 6–8) and confessions of faith (22:3–5, 9–11). The first complaint (22:1–2) expresses the psalmist's feelings of abandonment by God ("Why are you so far from helping me?"), while the second complaint (22:6–8) focuses on the shame that the speaker feels before other human beings ("scorned by others, and despised by the people") for having put trust in God. The first confession (22:3–5) reminds God that "in you our ancestors trusted" and "were not put to shame," while the second confession (22:9–11) recalls God's care for the psalmist throughout his life ("from the womb . . . on my mother's breast") and asks for help in the present crisis.

In 22:12–18 confession yields to complaint, with the complaints alternating between animal images (22:12–13, 16a) and first-person singular ("I") language (22:14–15, 16b). The animals—bulls, lions, and dogs—are fierce and threatening. The "I" statements express the physical sufferings of the speaker in various parts of his body: bones, heart, mouth, tongue, hands, and feet. Meanwhile his enemies are dividing up his clothes among themselves.

The petition (22:19–21a) joins all the themes together; the psalmist, calling God "my help" and "my aid," prays that God will come to his aid and not leave him forsaken. The psalmist prays that God will deliver him "from the power of the dog . . . from the mouth of the lion."

The final element—thanksgiving—in the "script" of the lament is developed at length in 22:21b–31. This second part of the psalm assumes that something good has already happened to the speaker. He has been rescued from "the horns of the wild oxen" (22:21b), thus continuing the pattern of animal images. The rescue is attributed to God's intervention in response to the petition: "he did not hide his face from me, but heard when I cried to him" (22:24).

The original setting for this thanksgiving appears to have been the Jerusalem temple, where the speaker is offering a thanksgiving to God. And so he calls upon those assembled with him to join in praising God and promises to share the food left over from the sacrifice with others: "The poor shall eat and be satisfied" (22:26).

From the Jerusalem temple the invitation to give thanks moves out in 22:27–31 to embrace the whole world ("All the ends of the earth"). The God of Israel "rules over the nations." The dominion of God even extends to the dead: "To him, indeed, shall all who sleep in the earth bow down" (22:29)—and it also extends to future generations who will themselves confess that "he has done it" (22:31).

Psalm 22 is clearly not a psalm of despair; rather, it is a psalm of hope and vindication. When early Christians sought to understand the mystery of Jesus' passion, death, and resurrection, they found in Psalm 22 a fitting "script." Thus the passion narratives by Mark and Matthew are full of allusions to Psalm 22, and the final words of Jesus are the first words of Psalm 22: "My God, my God, why have you forsaken me?" The Evangelists and other early Christians were more interested in showing how Jesus, in his passion, death, and resurrection, fulfilled God's will revealed in the Scriptures than they were in Jesus' feelings and psychology.

And yet speaking of Psalm 22 as a "script" should not take away from Jesus' total identification with the words of the psalm. Jesus' sufferings were real and intense, and the words of Psalm 22 served well to express his identity as a righteous sufferer who hoped for vindication by God. That Jesus had to struggle to accept the sufferings that he foresaw is expressed in his prayer in Gethsemane: "Abba, Father, for you all things are possible; remove this cup from me; yet, not what I want, but what you want" (Mark 14:36). The same theme is developed in Hebrews 5:7: "In the days of his flesh, Jesus offered up prayers and supplications, with loud cries and tears, to the one who was able to save him from death, and he was heard because of his reverent submission."

To appreciate the sufferings of Jesus we need to read the whole of Psalm 22. We cannot and should not disregard or eliminate the complaints and protests that are an integral part of the psalm. But we must also recognize that complaints about suffering do not preclude hope for vindication from God.

The Gloomiest Psalm

Psalm 88 has been called the "gloomiest" psalm. It contains an address and a petition, along with sustained sections of complaint. The confession of trust in God, if there is any at all, is subsumed into the address; instead, there is a challenge to God to do something. There is no talk of vindication or thanksgiving; indeed, the psalm ends on a note of "darkness." Nevertheless, the attention given to suffering is sufficient to justify classifying it as a lament.

After the address ("O LORD, God of my salvation"), the speaker begs that God will hear his prayer (88:1–2). The first section of complaint (88:3–9a) suggests that the speaker is close to death. For him (as for other Old Testament writers), life after death is at best a shadowy existence in Sheol, the abode of the dead. Many words and phrases in 88:3–7 express a gloomy view of life after death with such terms as "Sheol," "the Pit," "among the dead," "in the grave," and "in the regions dark and deep." To be dead is to be "cut off from your hand" (88:5). So desperate is the speaker's condition that he perceives himself to be "a thing of horror" (88:8) to his companions, and he himself feels trapped and miserable. The speaker blames God for his troubles: "Your wrath lies heavy upon me" (88:7).

Rather than professing trust in God as is the practice in most lament psalms, the speaker challenges God to intervene on his behalf (88:9b–12). The challenge focuses on the inability of the dead to praise God and the impossibility for God to perform wonders for the dead: "Do you work wonders for the dead? Do the shades rise up to praise you?" (88:10). The assumption is that "when you're dead, you're dead," and you can hardly be expected to join in proclaiming God's mighty acts or to be the object of divine favor anymore. So it is in God's own interest to save the psalmist. God's praise and honor are at stake.

The complaining resumes in 88:13–18 when the psalmist accuses God of refusing to hear his prayers. Again he contends that God is the source of his troubles, as he complains of "your terrors . . . your wrath . . . your dread." Again he contends that God has turned his friends against him. Overwhelmed by God and abandoned by his friends, he remains alone in his sufferings.

Besides being known as the gloomiest psalm, Psalm 88 is often called a dialogue with an absent God. The psalmist calls out to a God who appears to have abandoned him and to be hiding from him. Yet the absent God is still somehow present—present enough to be addressed in prayer, to be criticized, and to be angry at. Even though the psalmist feels that God has given up on him, he is not willing to give up on God. God exists. There is no speculative atheism or agnosticism here. God is the problem, and God had better do something about it. It is relatively easy to believe in God when things go well and life proceeds in an orderly way. In Psalm 88, however, we have someone whose life is a mess and God seems very far away. Somehow and from somewhere the psalmist is able to express a firm faith in God while challenging God and expressing anger at God.

This gloomy psalm, this dialogue with an absent God, is a great example of biblical spirituality. It gives a glimpse into an extraordinarily profound relationship with God. It shows how to pray when prayer seems most difficult: "O LORD, why do you cast me off? Why do you hide your face from me?" (88:14) It helps us to confront the reality of suffering and the terrifying experience of God's absence when God is most needed.

Possibilities and Problems

The lament psalms can provide the language and conceptuality for religious people to express themselves to God in the midst of suffering. They can give permission to take off the religious censor and to raise questions about God's possible roles in causing, allowing, or alleviating suffering. Their presence in the Jewish and Christian religious traditions means that the alienation and isolation that so many sufferers experience can be overcome.

The literary style in which the lament psalms were written has been described as "open and metaphorical." Thus they promote personal identification on the part of all kinds of people in very different times and places. The laments represent the largest category by far among the 150 canonical psalms. A partial list includes Psalms 3, 5, 6, 7, 13, 17, 22, 25, 26, 27, 28, 31, 35, 38, 39, 42, 43, 51, 53, 55, 56, 57, 61, 63, 64, 69, 70, 71, 86, 88, 102, 109, 120, 130, 140, 141, 142, and 143.

The lament psalms place suffering in the context of an ongoing personal and communal relationship with God. Most of them highlight God's fidelity and mighty acts in the past as the ground of hope for the future, and end on a note of praise and thanksgiving. As such, they provide positive resources for religious people who suffer.

Some problems associated with the lament psalms are obvious. These songs come from long ago (perhaps more than 2,500 years ago) and far away (ancient Israel's worship services at the Jerusalem temple). Moreover, calling upon God to "break the teeth of the wicked" (Psalm 3:7) seems excessively violent for modern religious sensibilities, however understandable such a wish may have been in the face of Israel's fierce enemies in the past.

At a deeper level, there is the problem that, while the lament psalms ask many good questions about suffering, they do not offer many good answers. With the exception of Psalm 88, they seldom push the issue as far as Job does. Furthermore, most of the lament psalms look back on past suffering. From the speaker's perspective the crisis has subsided, and now is the time to praise God and make a thanksgiving sacrifice. Indeed the primary purpose of the lament psalms is to proclaim the mighty acts of God in rescuing the speaker (or God's people) from suffering. They may not always express the feelings of people in the midst of suffering.

Questions for Reflection, Discussion, and Prayer

1. Recall one of your own experiences of suffering. What was the occasion? How did you react? Was your faith shaken or strengthened?

2. In light of the biblical laments, what does it mean to "cope" with suffering?

3. How do the literary conventions of the lament psalms reflect the actual religious experience of sufferers?

4. Does reading the whole of Psalm 22 affect your understanding of Jesus' passion, death, and resurrection?

5. What reactions do you have to Psalm 88? Does it depress you? Does it uplift you?

Chapter Two

The Law of Retribution

*I have lived a respectable, upstanding
life, my heart full of love for God. I
was once blessed with success, but never
boasted of it. My possessions were
extensive. My house was open to the
needy. I served God enthusiastically. . . .*
—Yossel Rakover

"**W**HY? WHY ME?" These questions emerge from
almost every human experience of suffering. Not
far behind is, "What did I (we) do wrong?" There
is a strong instinct in humans to seek the reason(s) for their suffering. And one reason that often emerges is that we have done
something wrong and so are getting what we deserve.

The need to search for the causes of suffering is deeply
engrained in us. Sometimes we find the answer and modify our
behavior in the light of bad experiences. But sometimes the
causes are beyond our knowledge or control, and the search
leads to increased frustration, misplaced guilt, or blaming others. And yet we find it hard to accept that we may never know
the real reason for our suffering.

One prominent biblical answer to our questions about the
cause of suffering is the law of retribution: The just are

rewarded and the wicked are punished. This principle can be found in one form or another in various parts of both Testaments, although there are also some discordant voices.

The practical advice given by the ancient sages of Israel often takes the law of retribution as a starting point, although Qoheleth and Job challenge its validity in every case. The Pentateuch and the Historical Books use it as a key to interpreting the history of Israel from Abraham to the exile of 587 B.C. The great prophets build on it as they warn and challenge the people of God to repent. The "original sin" of Adam and Eve brings various sufferings on the whole human race. Some texts in the New Testament (see Luke 13:1–5; John 9:3) seem to deny the law of retribution, but other texts (see Luke 18:28–30; Acts 5:1–11; 1 Corinthians 11:30) appear to uphold it.

The law of retribution runs through the Bible. And one of the reasons why many people accept the Bible as true and as God's word is that in many cases the law of retribution has proven true to human experience. I know that if I do something foolish such as putting my hand into a fire or stepping in front of an automobile, I will get hurt and suffer. I also believe that if I do good and avoid evil, I will (usually) lead a peaceful and happy life.

But the law of retribution does not prove true in all cases. And that is the major problem with it. In some cases, as with Job (or the Holocaust), it is not an adequate explanation for this particular human suffering. In using the Bible as a resource for understanding the mystery of suffering, we must bear in mind that the law of retribution is one (however prominent) among several biblical approaches. Enormous harm can be done when suffering persons persist in blaming themselves for things that are beyond their knowledge or control. Likewise, when suffering persons blame others and make them into enemies or scapegoats, the result is often an unending cycle of revenge, violence, and warfare.

The law of retribution—the righteous are rewarded and the wicked are punished—is only one biblical approach to suffering. Nevertheless, there is truth and wisdom to it, and so it deserves our attention. This chapter treats the law of retribution by starting with the Old Testament Wisdom Books, moving through the Pentateuch, the Historical Books, and the Prophets, and going backward to Adam and forward to Christ as the Second Adam.

The Way of Wisdom

The classic presentation of Israelite wisdom appears in the Book of Proverbs. The ancient wisdom movement was international in scope. And so it is possible to find close parallels to Proverbs in Egyptian, Mesopotamian, and Canaanite wisdom collections. These collections aim to present the solid results of reflection on human experience in the form of instructions ("my children") and proverbs (short sayings). The listeners are expected in turn to use these instructions and proverbs as guides to their own conduct.

Although part of the Hebrew Bible, the Book of Proverbs makes few explicit links to the Torah or to Israel's history. Rather, it seeks to distill the observations of the wise on human experience. These reflections in instruction and proverb form are not put forward as scientific laws that are valid in any and every circumstance. But they do seek to capture what has been the general or usual experience of human beings.

One of the great principles of the wisdom movement in its international manifestations and in its Israelite form is the law of retribution. It is generally true, according to the wisdom teachers, that wise and righteous behavior brings happiness, while foolish and evil conduct brings unhappiness, suffering, and death. In Israelite wisdom the intellectual (wise/fool) and the moral (righteous/unrighteous) dimensions go together. Since there is little or no concept of an afterlife, the rewards and punishments are understood to apply to one's life on earth.

The law of retribution is both an assumption and a theme in the Book of Proverbs. It can be found in one form or another in almost every chapter. A few examples from chapter 11 can illustrate the point. According to Proverbs 11:3, "The integrity of the upright guides them, but the crookedness of the treacherous destroys them." This proverb is built upon three contrasts: "integrity" versus "crookedness," "upright" versus "treacherous," and "guide" versus "destroy." The promise is that if you follow the way of wisdom and righteousness, your life will go smoothly. But if you move away from the path of wisdom and righteousness, you will harm yourself. The promise is that the righteous wise will prosper, whereas unrighteous fools will end up in disaster. With such a teaching there is always the temptation to reverse the sequence. That is, one is tempted to assume that those who end up in disaster must have been both foolish and wicked. This is the position of Job's "friends," as will be seen in the next chapter.

A second example of the law of retribution in proverb form is found in Proverbs 11:5: "The righteousness of the blameless keeps their ways straight, but the wicked fall by their own wickedness." In form and content this proverb repeats the previous one. Repetition was a positive value for the ancient sages in their instruction of young people on how to succeed in life.

The third example comes in Proverbs 11:8: "The righteous are delivered from trouble, and the wicked get into it instead." While "trouble" or distress may be part of everyone's life, the righteous person will either avoid it entirely or be easily extricated from it, while the wicked person falls into it ever more deeply and ends up being destroyed by it. For Proverbs and for most other ancient Near Eastern wisdom books, the law of retribution was generally true to human experience and so was a good guide to conduct and a way to happiness.

The biblical wisdom book known as Ecclesiastes or Qoheleth, however, expresses some skepticism about the truth of the law of retribution. Adopting the persona of King Solomon (the ideal Israelite sage), this author writing in the fourth or third century B.C. refuses to accept the assumption that people get what they deserve. The proverbs and instructions of the sages are supposed to be distillations of wisdom based on human experience. But Qoheleth's own experience casts doubt on the law of retribution. He observes that "there are righteous people who perish in their righteousness, and there are wicked people who prolong their life in their evildoing" (Ecclesiastes 7:15).

Qoheleth goes on to counsel moderation rather than putting too much emphasis on the law of retribution: "Do not be too righteous, and do not act too wise; why should you destroy yourself?" (7:16) By being obsessed with righteousness and wisdom, one can miss out on the pleasures of life. However, Qoheleth also recognizes that there is some truth in the law of retribution, and so he advises: "Do not be too wicked, and do not be a fool; why should you die before your time?" (7:17)

What especially renders questionable the law of retribution, according to Qoheleth, is the fact that everyone dies: "one fate comes to all" (9:2, 3). Death is the destiny of all humans, whether they are righteous or wicked, good or evil, clean or unclean, religiously observant or unobservant. And for Qoheleth there is no prospect of an afterlife or of rewards and punishments then. He says: "The dead know nothing; they have no more reward" (9:5). Human existence is always lived in the shadow of death: "the living know that they will die" (9:5). And human beings recognize the supreme value of life on earth and generally resist death in favor of prolonging their lives. That aspect of human experience is neatly expressed in a proverb: "a living dog is better than a dead lion" (9:4).

In his skepticism about the law of retribution, Qoheleth was a maverick within the international wisdom movement and within the Hebrew Bible. The early second-century B.C. wisdom teacher known as Ben Sira was a proponent of the more traditional wisdom teachings, including the law of retribution. In his huge wisdom book that is called Ecclesiasticus or Sirach, Ben Sira joined the Jewish wisdom movement to Israel's distinctive religious traditions of the Torah and salvation history. In fact,

Ben Sira seems to have been a teacher in a Jewish wisdom school associated with or at least very near the Jerusalem temple. In this respect Ben Sira was an important innovator.

Ben Sira accepted as true the basic assumptions that righteous and wise behavior leads to happiness, and that unrighteous and foolish behavior leads to unhappiness. Since he had no concept of rewards and punishments after death, the results of these behaviors must pertain to life on earth. In these matters Ben Sira agrees with Proverbs and other ancient Near Eastern wisdom writings.

At one point (Sirach 39:12–35), however, Ben Sira ventures into an area where other biblical writers do not go: the problem of "natural disasters" and the goodness of God's creation. Ben Sira states that "all the works of the Lord are very good" (39:16, see 39:33). He affirms God's sovereignty over creation and history: "whatever he commands will be done at the appointed time" (39:16). And he assumes that God's activity is always purposeful: "when he commands, his every purpose is fulfilled" (39:18).

Ben Sira's solution to the problem is moralistic and almost laughable. He contends that "from the beginning good things were created for the good, but for sinners good things and bad" (39:25). The basic necessities of life listed in 39:26 "are good for the godly, but for sinners they turn into evils" (39:27). The "natural disasters" brought about by winds, fire, hail, famine, and pestilence as well as wild animals and wars are interpreted as the instruments of God to punish the wicked. From this perspective, "everything proves good in its appointed time" (39:34). This solution enables Ben Sira to preserve the sovereignty and justice of God and the law of retribution in human affairs. But it leaves untouched the very serious problem of innocent suffering explored in the Book of Job. And it is open to the temptation of arguing backward from the occurrence of a natural or other wide-scale disaster to the sinfulness of the victims.

The Way of Israel's History

In the context of the Pentateuch (the first five books of the Old Testament) and the Historical Books (Joshua, Judges, 1 and 2 Samuel, and 1 and 2 Kings), the Book of Deuteronomy plays a pivotal role. It serves as the climax of the story of ancient Israel from the call of Abraham, through the exodus from Egypt and the wandering in the wilderness, to the entry into the promised land of Canaan. By his many exhortations and law-codes in the Book of Deuteronomy, Moses prepared the people for life in the promised land. The book also serves as the preamble or preface to Israel's history in the promised land from Joshua, the Judges, and the early kings, through the capture of the northern kingdom by the Assyrians, to the destruction of Jerusalem and its temple as well as the exile of its political and religious leaders in 587 B.C. Looking backward and forward, the Book of Deuteronomy provides a vantage point for interpreting ancient Israel's history in light of the law of retribution.

Near the end of the Book of Deuteronomy, Moses challenges the people to "choose life." They are about to enter the promised land. Moses tells them: "See, I have set before you today life and prosperity, death and adversity" (Deuteronomy 30:15). In the context of Moses' speech, to choose life means to keep the commandments or stipulations in Israel's covenant with the Lord God. The reward for observing these statutes will be God's blessing in the promised land. And so Moses says: "If you obey the commandments of the LORD your God that I am commanding you today, by loving the LORD your God, walking in his ways, and observing his commandments, decrees, and ordinances, then you shall live and become numerous, and the LORD your God will bless you in the land that you are entering to possess" (Deuteronomy 30:16).

Choosing life means obeying God's commandments, which in turn leads to God's blessing and prosperity. Choosing death means turning away from the Lord God and serving other gods, and this choice naturally leads to death and adversity: "I declare to you today that you shall perish; you shall not live long in the land that you are crossing the Jordan to enter and possess" (30:18). So choosing life (serving the Lord God and keeping his commandments) brings God's blessings and happiness. And choosing death (practicing idolatry and disregarding God's commandments) brings unhappiness and destruction. This is a religious, historical, and communal version of the law of retribution. Moses' challenge to the people of God in Deuteronomy 30:15–20 provides a lens to look backward at the Pentateuch and forward to the Historical Books. In fact, this text was most likely composed either after the exile of 587 B.C., or not long before it, when the Exile seemed to be a likely prospect. It was then placed in the mouth of Moses. In other words, Deuteronomy 30:15–20 is a prophecy after the fact. It was an attempt by the Deuteronomistic editor(s) to make sense out of what had happened in Israel's history and to provide a program for the renewal of Israel as God's people. From the perspective of Deuteronomy, Israel suffers because it failed to worship the Lord God properly and failed to keep God's commandments, and Israel prospers only when it observes God's law (the Torah).

Looking backward over the Pentateuch from the vantage point of Deuteronomy 30:15–20, one can see how God formed Israel into a people first through the patriarchs (Abraham, Isaac, and Jacob), then through the sojourn in Egypt and the Exodus under the leadership of Moses, and then after forty years of wandering in the wilderness up to Moses' final words.

The people are to interpret all 613 commandments in the Torah in the context of God's covenant relationship with Israel. They are the stipulations of God's covenant with Israel. They represent Israel's side of the covenant. If Israel observes these commandments as the revelation of God's will, it will be blessed and will prosper. All of the statutes are to be viewed in the framework of God's promise at Mount Sinai: "If you obey my voice and keep my covenant, you shall be my treasured possession out of all the peoples" (Exodus 19:5). On the contrary, if Israel sins by idolatry or rebellion or in some other way, it can expect suffering as the just punishment of God. The Torah defines wisdom and righteousness as God's commandments in the Torah, and applies the law of retribution to all Israel as God's people (and not just as individuals).

The early history of Israel in the land of Canaan according to Joshua and Judges is interpreted in the light of its covenant relationship. Israel wins great victories not by its military superiority but by the hand of God. And it fails when it departs from the Torah. And when one person (Achan) in Joshua 7 defies God's ban on taking the spoils of war, the entire people suffers for his sins: "the people of Israel broke faith in regard to the devoted things . . . and the anger of the LORD burned against the people of Israel" (Joshua 7:1).

The biblical narratives about the kings of Israel and Judah in 1 and 2 Samuel and in 1 and 2 Kings are full of great stories and valuable historical information. Yet all these accounts are presented in the editorial framework of the law of retribution as interpreted in Deuteronomy. As in the final edition of the Pentateuch, the Torah provides the way of wisdom and righteousness, and what is at stake is the collective identity of Israel as the people of God. Measured by these criteria, almost all the kings of Israel and Judah are judged negatively. The editorial assessment of Jehoiakim, one of the last kings of Judah, is typical: "He did what was evil in the sight of the LORD, just as his ancestors had done" (2 Kings 23:37).

From Solomon to the Exile in 587 B.C. the most persistent and harmful sin on the part of Israel's kings was idolatry, according to the judgment of the Deuteronomist. The kings' persistent failures to worship the God of Israel and their participation in pagan cults affected negatively the fortunes of the whole people. And, of course, it was tempting to reverse the process and to reason from the misfortunes of the people to the sins of their kings.

The Pentateuch and the Historical Books offer a religious and moral reading of Israel's history from Abraham to the Exile.

The cultural, political, social, and economic factors that are so important in modern historiography are of secondary interest at best. These writings interpret that history in the light of Israel's defeats and failures, and trace them back to the sins of the people and of their kings. And they present a constructive program for the renewal of God's people: Follow the Torah as God's way of wisdom and righteousness, and avoid the sins of pre-exilic Israel and their just punishments.

The Way of Israel's Prophets

The interpretation of ancient Israel's history in terms of the law of retribution had its roots in the warnings of the great prophets. For example (and there are very many examples), the prophet Isaiah challenged the people of Judah to choose life: "If you are willing and obedient, you shall eat the good of the land; but if you refuse and rebel, you shall be devoured by the sword" (Isaiah 1:19–20). Likewise, the prophet Jeremiah told the people of Jerusalem: "Your wickedness will punish you, and your apostasies will convict you" (Jeremiah 2:19). And Ezekiel blamed the capture of Jerusalem and the destruction of the temple on the people's sins: "And because of all your abominations, I [God] will do to you what I have never yet done" (Ezekiel 5:9). The Book of Lamentations also linked the city's destruction to wrongdoing on the people's part: "Jerusalem sinned grievously, so she has become a mockery" (Lamentations 1:8). All the prophets agree in invoking the law of retribution as a way of explaining the greatest catastrophes in the history of ancient Israel.

And yet the prophets refuse to give sin and suffering the last word. Rather, they hold out a hope of repentance and restoration for God's people. Writing in the late eighth century B.C., Isaiah looked forward to a new king who would be "Emmanuel" ("God with us") and would usher in a peaceful kingdom (see Isaiah 7:14, 11:1–9). Jeremiah foresaw the possibility of a "new covenant" written on the hearts of God's people (see

Jeremiah 31:31–34). And Ezekiel in chapters 40–48 laid out a verbal blueprint for the New Jerusalem.

The prophets also taught that the enemies of Judah who served as God's instruments for punishing the people for their sins would themselves be punished for their own sins and their arrogance. Moreover, for the prophets, the suffering of God's people is not endless. Rather, they found in the concept of a "remnant" within Israel the principle of continuity with regard to Israel's identity as the people of God. While Ezekiel insisted on the collective guilt of the exile generation, he rejected the fatalistic idea of inherited guilt expressed in this proverb: "The parents have eaten sour grapes, and the children's teeth are set on edge." Rather, Ezekiel emphasized that sinners will die for their own sins but the righteous among God's people can escape the cycle of sin and punishment (see Ezekiel 18:1–4, 19–20).

The prophets (like the Deuteronomists) offered a religious and moral interpretation of the events leading up to the great catastrophe of 587 B.C. According to them, the destruction of Jerusalem was an appropriate punishment for the people's sins (especially idolatry) and so was a manifestation of the sovereignty and justice of the God of Israel. And yet the same prophets portray the God of Israel as unfailingly faithful, loving, and caring toward his people. And so it is always possible for God's people to repent and begin over. For them, the suffering that is just punishment for sin is neither inevitable nor eternal. Rather, as Isaiah 40–55 (Second Isaiah) shows, the return from exile and the restoration of God's people in its holy city could be a new exodus and even a new creation. Sin and suffering do not have the last word.

The Way of Adam

The first and most famous biblical case of suffering as punishment for sin comes in Genesis 3, with the "original sin" of Adam and Eve. God's one command to the first couple was that they should not eat or even touch the fruit of the tree in the middle of the garden, or "you shall die" (Genesis 3:3). The serpent, however, convinces them that if they do eat the fruit of the tree, "you will be like God, knowing good and evil" (3:4). And so they ate, and "the eyes of both were opened" (3:7). The consequences or punishments for their disobedience involved suffering of various kinds: shame at nakedness, fear of snakes, pain in childbirth, a woman's subordination to her husband, the pain of hard work, and death ("you are dust, and to dust you shall return," 3:19).

Behind the story of the first sin is the law of retribution. God set forth a commandment and promised a punishment ("you shall die"). Adam and Eve transgressed the commandment and so suffered the consequences of their disobedience. The claim of Genesis 3 is that the consequences of this first sin are visited upon all humans. The "original sin" is thus the common lot of all humankind. Interpreters through the centuries have explained the inherited consequences of original sin in various ways. For some, it is like a genetically transmitted disease handed on from generation to generation. For others, it means that all humans repeat the disobedience of Adam and Eve. For still others, Genesis 3 is the result of reasoning backward from human suffering (shame, pain in childbirth, hard work, and death) to its cause in the disobedient action of our first ancestors. What is common to these different approaches is the idea that the consequences of "original sin" affect every human being.

One of the great themes of Genesis 1–11 is the spread of sin and its consequences. The "original sin" is followed in turn by Cain's murder of Abel (Genesis 4:1–16), the general wickedness of humankind that leads to the flood (Genesis 6:1–7), and the human arrogance demonstrated in building the Tower of Babel (Genesis 11:1–9). By choosing Abraham to form "a great nation" (see Genesis 12:1–3), God in effect makes a new beginning and seeks to rescue humankind from the reign of sin and death.

It is curious how little attention is given to Adam's sin in the rest of the Hebrew Bible. It is never cited as the explanation for Israel's sin and suffering. Even in Jewish works from the New Testament period, there is likely to be more attention given to the "evil inclination" within the human person or to the "fall of the angels" (see Genesis 6:1–4) than to Adam's sin as a way of explaining sin and suffering.

In the New Testament, it was Paul (especially in Romans 5:12–21) who developed the theme of Adam's sin and the parallels (and differences) between Adam and Christ. With Adam's sin the power of "sin" and its consequence "death" entered the world and exercised dominion over all humans. With Adam's sin came disobedience, condemnation, and death. But Jesus, through his death and resurrection, overcame the power of sin and death. Of course, these two "powers" still exist but they need no longer exercise their dominion or compulsion over human beings. With Christ came the possibility of obedience to God, justification or acquittal from sin, and eternal life.

As Paul says, "the free gift is not like the trespass" (Romans 5:15). The transgression was Adam's sin, and the gift or grace was Christ. According to Paul, God in Christ has offered to all humans the possibility of escaping the consequences of Adam's sin: "Therefore we have been buried with him by baptism into death, so that, just as Christ was raised from the dead by the glory of the Father, so we too might walk in newness of life" (Romans 6:4). Sin and suffering do not have the last word. Rather, Jesus' life, death, and resurrection have made it possible for all humans (not just the people of Israel) to find freedom from the power of sin and death and to enjoy right relationship with God. Christ has reversed the process begun by Adam's sin and overcome its deadly consequences.

Possibilities and Problems

The law of retribution—the righteous are rewarded and the wicked are punished—often proves true not only in the Bible but also in our human experience. Just as the biblical writers

used it to explain ordinary human existence and the history of
God's people, so one need only look at a daily newspaper to see
terrible suffering being brought about by human sin and the
happiness that results from just and loving conduct. Furthermore, when persons come to see the real reasons for their suffering and recognize that they can do something about them,
they frequently begin to take responsibility for their harmful
behaviors and seek to change the direction of their lives.

However, the law of retribution does not always prove
true. The great problem is trying to discern whether it applies
in this or that particular case of suffering. Many experiences of
suffering are so complex that they defy the easy explanation
that the law of retribution gives. Why does this person get can-
cer? Why do those people die or lose all their possessions in a
fire or a flood? It may be possible to find answers in some cases
(such as smoking, careless use of matches, or building too close
to the seashore). But all too often our search for causes is in
vain. And what is really gained by obsessing over causes while
failing to deal with the suffering itself?

An especially persistent and dangerous human tendency
is to reverse the terms of the law of retribution and make it say:
"Those who suffer must have sinned, and those who prosper
must be righteous and wise." The connection between suffering and sin is very powerful in the minds of many religious
people. For example, on meeting a man who was blind from
birth, Jesus' disciples ask him: "Rabbi, who sinned, this man or
his parents, that he was born blind?" (John 9:2) Jesus answers
that none of them sinned and that the man's blindness will
serve as the occasion in which "God's works might be revealed
in him" (John 9:3).

As an explanation for suffering, the law of retribution
focuses principally on the victims. Of course, one might attrib-
ute the suffering to the wrath of God against human sinfulness
or to demonic forces having power over humans. But most religious people take for granted the omnipotence and the justice
of God. It is these assumptions that are examined critically in

what is the fullest biblical investigation of the mystery of suffering—the Book of Job.

Questions for Reflection, Discussion, and Prayer

1. Can you recall a personal experience of suffering when the law of retribution proved true, and one when it proved false?

2. Which makes more sense to you: the sayings in Proverbs 11 or the skepticism of Qoheleth? How do you assess Ben Sira's attempt at explaining "natural disasters"?

3. How valid is the religious and moral reading of ancient Israel's history in the Old Testament?

4. Does "original sin" help you to understand some aspects of human suffering? Which ones?

5. What theological modifications does the law of retribution undergo in the various parts of the Bible?

Chapter Three

The Mystery of Suffering: The Book of Job

*This, however, does not mean that the
pious members of my family should
justify the edict, saying that God
and His judgments are correct.*
—Yossel Rakover

THE BOOK OF JOB is the longest sustained exploration of
the mystery of suffering in the Bible. The main character, a man named Job, is the model of biblical piety, perfectly righteous and pious. Nevertheless, he is subjected to
great physical and personal sufferings. He loses his possessions
and his children. He is afflicted with a terrible skin disease. His
relatives, friends, and servants shun him. People whom he once
despised make sport of him. Perhaps his most intense suffering,
however, is his inability to understand why he is suffering. He
had done nothing wrong.

At the beginning Job shows remarkable patience in
accepting his sufferings from the hand of God. But the patient
Job soon yields to Job the relentless complainer and seeker after
truth. Whether Job finds the truth depends on how one interprets the ambiguous ending of the book.

The conversations between Job and his friends reveal the problems associated with the law of retribution. Job's friends assume that because he is suffering he must have sinned—and so they advise him from many different perspectives to confess his sin and rely on God's mercy. Job, however, maintains his innocence and contends that the real problem lies not with him but with God. Since Job does not question the omnipotence of God, he argues that God is being unjust in his case. What is at stake is the nature of divine justice: Is it really the same as human justice? Is God bound to our rules? Who makes the rules of justice?

The Book of Job is great literature. The prose account about Job in the prologue (1:1–2:13) and the epilogue (42:7–17) effectively evokes a setting long ago and far away. The magnificent poetry in the speeches from Job, his three friends, Elihu, and God joins form and content in a courageous theological investigation of the mystery of innocent suffering.

The Book of Job

The overall structure of the Book of Job is clear. The prologue (chaps. 1–2) sets the scene: The righteous and pious Job loses his property and undergoes intense physical suffering. The arrival of his three "friends"—Eliphaz, Bildad, and Zophar—to comfort Job provides the occasion for three sets of debates between them and Job about why Job is suffering (chaps. 3–14, 15–21, 22–31), followed by an intervention by still another "comforter" named Elihu (chaps. 32–37). The book reaches its climax with God's speeches from the whirlwind (38:1–42:6). The epilogue (42:7–17) tells about the restoration of Job's health and prosperity.

The prologue and epilogue appear in standard Hebrew prose and present few problems to translators. The rest of the book, however, contains perhaps the most difficult and the most beautiful poetry in the Hebrew Bible. Large sections have defied the linguistic skills of the greatest biblical scholars both in antiquity and in the modern era. Some have even speculated that the poetic parts were originally composed in a language other than Hebrew—Aramaic or Edomite. At any rate, the Hebrew text of most of the book presents many difficulties for translators, as a comparison of several modern translations will show.

In discussing the date of the Book of Job, one must distinguish between its literary setting, cultural background, and time of composition. The literary setting is long ago (before Moses it seems) and far away ("the land of Uz"—otherwise unknown). The cultural background is the international wisdom movement and its distinctive manifestation in the land of Israel, even though the book takes a critical stance toward some of its basic principles. The actual time of composition is generally placed between the sixth and fourth centuries B.C. This dating sets the work in the context of a great crisis in biblical history: the destruction of Jerusalem and its temple in 587 B.C., and the exile of Judah's leaders to Babylon. However, if this is so, one might expect some direct references (or even allusions) to those catastrophes. Job may well be a figure symbolic of Israel's collective suffering in the sixth century B.C. But nothing in the text indicates that he is even Jewish. Rather, he is portrayed as a "foreigner" who lived before the gift of the Torah to Moses on Mount Sinai and outside the land of Israel. And so the precise historical circumstances of the book's composition remain vague.

The purpose of the Book of Job is to explore the theme of innocent suffering and the various attempts at explaining it. The innocent and righteous Job is suffering greatly. Does Job deserve this? His "friends" assume the truth of the law of retribution. Since Job is suffering, they assume that he must have sinned. They imagine that they are upholding and defending God's omnipotence and justice. However, Job is certain that he has not sinned, and so he reasons that God is the source of his problems. The friends blame Job, and Job blames God and the friends.

The Book of Job is by far the most sustained biblical exploration of the mystery of suffering and the problem of theodicy. The problem is how to affirm simultaneously the truth of three propositions: God is all powerful; God is just; and Job is innocent of evildoing. The book exposes the weaknesses of taking the law of retribution as the only explanation of suffering. In doing so it opens up for investigation the mystery of innocent suffering.

THE PROLOGUE (1–2): The prose prologue sets the scene for the poetic speeches that follow. It introduces the main characters and explains how Job came to suffer.

The description of Job in 1:1–5 insists on his complete righteousness: "That man was blameless and upright, one who feared God and turned away from evil" (1:1). Job's large family of seven sons and three daughters as well as his many possessions are signs of God's favor toward him. And so pious is Job that he offers sacrifices every day on the chance that one of his children may have sinned.

Job's perfect life is interrupted by two tests (1:6–22 and 2:1–10) that result in his suffering. Each test consists of a heavenly scene and an earthly scene. The first test begins in the heavenly court (1:6–12) where God points out to Satan "my servant Job" and boasts of Job's righteousness. Satan replies that God has made things too easy for Job and proposes that he undergo as a test the loss of his possessions: "touch all that he has, and he will curse you to your face" (1:11). The test is executed on earth (1:13–22) as a series of messengers report to Job about the loss of his livestock, servants, and sons and daughters. In response, Job affects the garb and posture of lament and utters a profession of his perfect acceptance of suffering: "Naked I came from my mother's womb, and naked shall I return there; the LORD gave, and the LORD has taken away; blessed be the name of the LORD" (1:21).

The second test also begins in the heavenly court (2:1–6) where God once more boasts about Job. This time Satan proposes that Job himself should suffer physical pain: "touch his bone and his flesh, and he will curse you to your face" (2:5).

The test is executed on earth (2:7–10) where Job is afflicted with terrible sores "from the sole of his foot to the crown of his head" (2:7). Again Job shows himself to be the model of patient acceptance when he explains to his wife: "Shall we receive the good at the hand of God, and not receive the bad?" (2:10)

Three friends—Eliphaz, Bildad, and Zophar—arrive in 2:11–13 to console and comfort Job. They sit with him for seven days. They join in Job's posture of lament and show great sensitivity toward him: "no one spoke a word to him, for they saw that his suffering was very great" (2:13).

As the book proceeds, the behavior of the human characters will change. In his two responses to the tests (1:21; 2:10), Job interprets his sufferings as a part of human existence. Though mysterious, his suffering is not unexpected (although his lack of concern for the fate of his children is puzzling). But the "patient" Job will turn into a relentless complainer, while the "sensitive" friends will become Job's accusers.

In the prologue Satan has been true to his name, which means "accuser." He serves as both challenger and provocateur. But then Satan disappears entirely. The most problematic figure, however, is God. In the two tests God seems to be playing games with Job's life. He allows Satan to oversee the destruction of Job's household and Job's personal physical sufferings. Yet he puts the blame on Satan: "you incited me against him, to destroy him for no reason" (2:3). God will be silent until chapter 38, and whether he really answers Job's questions remains a matter of dispute.

THE SPEECHES (3–31): The mood changes when Job issues his "howl" in chapter 3, which in turn provokes his "friends" to try to engage him in conversation. There are three rounds (chaps. 4–14, 15–21, 22–31) in which each of the three friends speaks in turn and Job responds. In fact, these conversations seldom reach the level of dialogue. Instead, Job and his friends generally talk past one another and, near the end, the talk becomes chaotic. The speeches of the friends bring forward all the standard arguments about suffering, while Job continues to maintain his innocence and blame God. They become repetitious, incoherent, and boring. All this talk about suffering is necessary but ultimately fruitless.

Job's lament in chapter 3 provides the occasion for the dialogues. What Job says seems so outrageous to his friends that they feel compelled to respond. In his "howl" Job first curses the day on which he was born (3:3–5) and the night in which he was conceived (3:6–10). He issues six curses against that day ("let that day be darkness") and nine curses against that night ("let thick darkness seize it"). Then in 3:11–26 Job keeps asking "why" he was born at all (see 3:11, 12, 16, 20, 23) and looks longingly upon death as offering the only true rest from his troubles. By contrast, his present life of suffering is full of anxiety: "I am not at ease, nor am I quiet; I have no rest; but trouble comes" (3:26).

In his first speech (chaps. 4–5), Eliphaz puts forward most of the standard explanations for suffering. While they were current in ancient Near Eastern wisdom circles, each of us has heard them many times in our own lives and probably said them ourselves. Eliphaz begins by telling Job to stop his whining. Even though Job had counseled many others in their suffering, now that suffering has come to him he is "impatient" and "dismayed" (4:5). Next, in 4:6, Eliphaz tells Job to have confidence in God and his own integrity, and to take them as the ground of his hope. If Job is truly righteous before God, he has no reason to be afraid: "Think now, who that was innocent ever perished?" (4:7)

In 4:17–21 Eliphaz takes the discussion in a very different direction without showing any sense that he may be contradicting himself. In 4:17 he asks, "Can mortals be righteous before God?" Since he expects a negative answer, it follows that suffering is part of the sinful human condition. He goes on to reaffirm the law of retribution with regard to individual human beings: "Surely vexation kills the fool, and jealousy slays the simple" (5:2). Next he urges Job to recommit himself to God as the powerful and just one: "as for me, I would seek God, and to

God would I commit my cause" (5:8). Then he takes up the idea of suffering as a divine discipline: "How happy is the one whom God reproves; therefore do not despise the discipline of the Almighty" (5:17). Finally, Eliphaz counsels patience in the present because this suffering will surely pass and Job's life will be restored to harmony and happiness.

Eliphaz has "said it all." His words from 2,500 years ago are still current—and still unsatisfying to innocent sufferers like Job. There is truth in all of his considerations and, in the face of the mystery of suffering, it is hard to refrain from repeating them. But they fail to impress Job.

Whereas Eliphaz seems convinced that Job is the problem, Job, in chapter 6, contends that God and his friends constitute the real problem. For him God is the real cause of his suffering: "For the arrows of the Almighty are in me" (6:4). Job's best hope is that God might crush him and so put an end to his suffering (see 6:9). The advice given by his friends seems superficial and proceeds from their own fear of suffering: "you see my calamity, and are afraid" (6:21). What Job really wants from them (and from God) is the reason for his suffering: "Teach me, and I will be silent. Make me understand how I have gone wrong" (6:24).

In chapter 7 Job presents his own reflections on the human condition. Their content can be summarized by the old bumper-sticker slogan, "Life's a bitch, and then you die." From Job's perspective human existence is a kind of slavery ("hard service") that is lived out in anxiety and in physical decay, and comes to an end "without hope" (7:6). The best thing about death is that then God will cease to spy on Job ("The eye that beholds me will see me no more," 7:8). For Job, death is the end of human existence ("those who go down to Sheol do not come up," 7:9), and he has no desire for eternal life: "I loathe my life; I would not live forever" (7:16).

Job ends his first speech in 7:17–21 with what seems to be a parody on Psalm 8 ("what are human beings that you are mindful of them, mortals that you care for them?"). Whereas

Psalm 8 marvels at the great dignity of human beings and at
God's special care for them, Job wishes that God would show
less care for him. He would prefer a distant and uninvolved God
to the "watcher of humanity" and wonders why God is so concerned with the sins of human beings. Job's only escape from
this too watchful God is death, when "you will seek me, but I
shall not be" (7:21).

When Bildad, in chapter 8, defends God's justice and urges
Job to repent (he must have sinned—otherwise he would not be
suffering), Job, in chapters 9–10, introduces a theme that will
run through his speeches: his search for a fair trial before God.
His problem is "how can a mortal be just before God?" (9:2) But
Job's formulation here is not so much an appeal to human sinfulness as it is to the unjust situation in which God appears to him
to be both judge and adversary. He accuses God of being capri-
cious and elusive (see 9:5–7, 11). While defending his own innocence ("I am blameless," 9:21), he accuses God of injustice ("he
destroys both the blameless and the wicked," 9:22).

And yet in his search for justice, Job has nowhere else to go.
If he lays aside his complaint, people will assume that he is guilty
(9:27–28). If he does penance, he is admitting fault (9:30–31).
Since God is both judge and adversary, there is no neutral party
("umpire") to guarantee that justice will be done in Job's case.

Nevertheless, Job cannot resist preparing his legal case. In
chapter 10 he rehearses how he will approach God: "I will say
to God, Do not condemn me; let me know why you contend
against me" (10:2). Echoing his earlier complaints, Job wants to
know why God, who showed such care in bringing Job into life,
should now be tormenting him to the point that he prays: "Let
me alone, that I may find a little comfort" (10:20).

When Zophar, in chapter 11, criticizes Job for asking
impossible questions and urges Job to confess his sins, Job calls
into question the assumption that God is a wise and just governor of the universe (chap. 12) and renews his search for a fair
trial: "But I would speak to the Almighty, and I desire to argue
my case with God" (13:3).

In chapter 13 Job begins to lay out his legal case. First in 13:6–12 he dismisses the charges of his friends as arising from a mistaken assumption that they are defending God: "Will you speak falsely for God, and speak deceitfully for him?" (13:7) Then he declares his intention to "defend my ways to his face" (13:15) and asks God to tell him the reason for his suffering: "How many are my iniquities and my sins? Make me know my transgression and my sin" (13:23). Job's complaint is that God is punishing him without telling him what the formal charges are against him. In his imaginary legal case, Job remains confident of his own innocence, and so he questions the justice of God.

And yet according to chapter 14, Job has little real hope of getting a fair trial for himself. As he reflects on the human condition ("few of days and full of trouble," 14:1), he observes that there is more hope for a tree (which when cut down sprouts to life again) than there is for a human being (who dies and remains dead). No sooner does Job raise up a tiny hope for life after death in 14:13–17 than he dashes it down again and blames God in the process: "so you destroy the hope of mortals" (14:19). For humans, death is the ultimate experience of loneliness: "They feel only the pain of their own bodies, and mourn only for themselves" (14:22).

When Eliphaz, in chapter 15, accuses Job of arrogance before God and unwillingness to admit his own sinfulness, Job, in chapter 16, responds that God, not Job, is the real problem: "Surely now God has worn me out; he has made desolate all my company" (16:7). From Job's perspective it is not simply a case of God's allowing him to suffer. Rather, God is the agent or cause of his suffering. Job makes this charge with the help of very violent images: "I was at ease, and he broke me in two; he seized me by the neck and dashed me to pieces; he set me up as his target; his archers surround me. He slashes open my kidneys, and shows no mercy; he pours out my gall on the ground" (16:12–13). In the face of such a powerful adversary (who is also his judge), Job concludes that all hope is futile: "where then is my hope? Who will see my hope?" (17:15)

When Bildad, in chapter 18, contends that the wicked bring their suffering upon themselves, Job, in chapter 19, again points the finger at God for causing his suffering ("He breaks me down on every side," 19:10), and for leaving him isolated ("My breath is repulsive to my wife, I am loathsome to my own family," 19:17).

And yet a spark of hope still remains within Job: "For I know that my Redeemer lives, and that at the last he will stand upon the earth" (19:27). In ancient Israel a "redeemer" (*go'el*) acted on behalf of a relative to buy back family property (see Leviticus 25:25), to exact vengeance (see Numbers 35:19–21), or to marry a widow (see Ruth). This is another example of Job's desire for a patron or protector. Christians instinctively think of Jesus as this Redeemer and as the fulfillment of Job's wish. But in the historical context of the book's composition, the verse most likely refers to God. In this hope against hope, Job wishes that God would take his side and vindicate his innocence.

From this point onward the conversation becomes even more repetitious, with Job and his friends repeating the same arguments. When Zophar claims that "the exulting of the wicked is short" (20:5), Job responds that "the wicked live on, reach old age, and grow mighty in power" (21:7). When Eliphaz charges that Job must have sinned ("there is no end to your iniquities," 22:5) and urges him to "return to the Almighty" (22:23), Job replies that God has become inaccessible to him: "If I go forward, he is not there; or backward, I cannot perceive him" (23:8). In chapters 24 to 27 it is often difficult to know who is saying what to whom. Some textual problems and dislocations contribute to the chaotic nature of the conversation. Rational discourse about suffering and theodicy has broken down.

The necessary "time out" is supplied by a beautiful poem in chapter 28 about the search for wisdom. The first part of the poem (28:1–11) reflects on the extraordinary ability of human beings to search out the most obscure places on earth and to find silver, gold, and other precious metals. The search for wisdom, however, is more difficult: "But where shall wisdom be found? And where is the place of understanding?" (28:12) Humans do not know where wisdom is or how they can get there. Wisdom surpasses everything else in value, but wisdom cannot be purchased. Only God knows where wisdom is: "God understands the way to it, and he knows its place" (28:23). Meanwhile for human beings the only way to wisdom is "the fear of the Lord . . . and to depart from evil" (28:28).

Job's final speech in chapters 29–31 begins with a remembrance of the past in which he reflects on how wonderful his life was before his suffering began. Then God watched over him at home: "the friendship of God was upon my tent" (29:4). And when he went to the city gate, he received great respect: "the young men saw me and withdrew, and the aged rose up and stood" (29:8). Job was the embodiment of virtue: "I put on righteousness, and it clothed me; my justice was like a robe and a turban" (29:14). Then people looked to Job for advice and leadership, and he dispensed it as a benefactor—"a king among his troops, like one who comforts mourners" (29:25). Job was truly "the great man." Viewed from the perspective of his present suffering, everything about Job's past life seemed perfect— a common reaction among suffering people.

In the present, however, Job's life appears totally miserable (chap. 30). Those people whom Job once despised now make sport of him (30:1–11). He has lost all honor and reputation and is full of fear and anxiety (30:12–18) because God "has cast me into the mire, and I have become like dust and ashes" (30:19). Once more, in 30:20–31, Job recites his familiar complaints: God is his enemy; his own actions of compassion have not been rewarded; and he lives now in misery.

Job's obsession with laying out his legal case before God reaches its climax in chapter 31. By way of introduction, Job states as his assumption the principle of retribution: "Does not calamity befall the unrighteous, and disaster the workers of iniquity?" (31:3) He also affirms the omnipotence of God: "Does he not see my ways, and number all my steps?" (31:4) Then in a long series of "If . . . then" statements, Job presents a catalogue of sins (deceit, covetousness, adultery, injustice, lack of compassion, greed, idolatry, and so on) and lists the punishments appropriate to them. The point is that Job has committed none of these sins and so he should not undergo suffering as punishments for them.

What Job really wants from God is an indictment, a reason for his suffering: "Oh, that I had the indictment written by my adversary!" (31:35) If only Job knew why he was suffering, he would carry his indictment around on his shoulders and wear it like a crown. At least then he would understand what was happening to him. In Job's perspective there must be some hidden reason for his suffering, or God is unjust.

ELIHU'S INTERVENTION (32–37): At the end of a long and frustrating meeting it often happens that someone who has said nothing stands up and condemns everyone else for wasting time and not dealing with "the real issue." In the Book of Job that someone is Elihu. His intervention takes the form of four speeches (chaps. 32–33, 34, 35, 36–37). Elihu's monologues break the flow and are cast in a somewhat different language and style. There is no response from Job. Some argue that these speeches have been added to the original composition by the author or by a later editor. In their present position they prepare Job (and us) for God's intervention and monologue in chapters 38–41. They do, however, make some fresh points about how God speaks to humans, about God's justice and purpose in creation, and about suffering as a divine discipline.

In 32:1–5 Elihu bursts on to the scene, ready to explode with anger. He is angry at Job "because he justified himself rather than God" (32:2) and at Job's friends because "they had found no answer" (32:3). Out of deference to his elders, Elihu had remained silent. But now he can remain silent no longer.

In his first speech (32:6–33:33) Elihu begins by claiming his right to speak. In 32:6–22 he explains that he has listened respectfully to his elders and has been disappointed at their failure to answer Job. Now "full of words" (32:18) and "ready to burst" (32:19), Elihu is compelled to speak. In 33:9–11 Elihu neatly summarizes Job's case: Job maintains his innocence ("I am clean, without transgression") and blames God for his sufferings ("he [God] counts me as his enemy"). Then Elihu sets out to refute Job's claim that God is distant and absent. Rather, Elihu contends that God does speak to humans in dreams (33:15–18) and especially in serious illnesses and other "near death" experiences (33:19–21). As humans face the prospect of death ("the Pit") they turn to God and confess their sins, and God accepts them back. Elihu here alludes to the dynamic of the lament psalms in which the speaker recounts how God brought rescue from "near death": "He has redeemed my soul from going down to the Pit, and my life shall see the light" (33:28). Elihu's implication is that Job should regard his present suffering as an opportunity to turn back to God. In and through Job's suffering, God is speaking to Job, and Job should listen.

In his second speech (chap. 34) Elihu again neatly summarizes Job's claims that he is innocent and God is unjust (34:5–6), only to dismiss them as untrue. He launches into an extended defense of God's justice ("far be it from God that he should do wickedness," 34:10) and of the law of retribution ("according to their deeds he will repay them," 34:11). Behind Elihu's remarks is the suggestion that since Job is suffering, he must have sinned. God, however, as the creator and sustainer of the universe, must be its just governor: "Shall one who hates justice govern?" (34:17) Moreover, God is omniscient ("he sees all their steps," 34:21) and makes sure that the wicked are punished. Elihu implies that if Job would confess his sin, it would go well for him. Meanwhile he dismisses Job as one who "speaks without knowledge" (34:35) and "adds rebellion to his sin" (34:37).

In his third speech (chap. 35) Elihu takes up Job's complaints about God's absence or silence by appealing to God's transcendence. According to Elihu, God is beyond being harmed by human transgressions or being helped by their righteous deeds. These deeds pertain more to humans themselves than to God (35:5–8). Then Elihu suggests that most humans call on God in prayer only when they find themselves in trouble. But if they neglect the praise of God in good times, why should they expect God to answer their cries in bad times? Again Elihu dismisses Job's complaints as "an empty cry" (35:13) and scolds him for his "empty talk" (35:16).

In his fourth speech (chaps. 36–37) Elihu again defends God's just governance of the world and offers reflections on the positive value of suffering. The theme of suffering as divine discipline is developed especially in 36:8–15: "He delivers the afflicted by their affliction, and opens their ear by adversity" (36:15). The idea is that suffering can be a message or instruction from God (what we term "a wake-up call") to turn away from destructive behavior toward a better way of life. Elihu admits that perfect knowledge of God is beyond human comprehension: "Surely God is great, and we do not know him" (36:26). Nevertheless, reflection on "the wondrous works of God" (37:14) will confirm, according to Elihu, that God "is great in power and justice, and abundant righteousness he will not violate" (37:23).

Elihu does make some fresh points about how God speaks to humans, about God's justice and purpose in creation, and about suffering as a divine discipline. And yet he follows his older colleagues in blaming Job and defending God. He claims to want to help Job, but he continues to treat Job's suffering as an intellectual problem to be solved. And so despite Elihu's new points, not much progress has been made in the debate. What is needed is a new perspective.

GOD'S SPEECHES (38–41): Throughout the book Job has asked that God give him "the real reason" for his suffering. Job has maintained his innocence. He has never doubted the omnipotence of God. His main concern has been with the justice of God: How could a just God cause him so much suffering? At last, in chapters 38–41, God speaks. But God does not give Job the real reason for his suffering. Instead, God offers Job a different perspective.

There are two speeches from God. The first speech (chaps. 38–39) reflects on God's power over (and care for) the cosmos and the animal kingdom. The second speech (40:6–41:34) focuses on God's power (and care for) Behemoth and Leviathan—two "monsters" with godlike powers. In these speeches God does not give answers. Rather, God asks questions that have the effect of overwhelming Job. The dynamic is set at the start: "I will question you, and you shall declare to me" (38:3). At the end of each speech there is a brief response from Job (40:1–5, 42:1–6). In fact, Job is left speechless.

The first speech (chaps. 38–39) concerns God's governance of the cosmos and of the animal kingdom. The tone is set by God's first question to Job: "Were you there when I laid the foundation of the earth?" (38:4) The obvious answer is, "No." With these questions God is inviting Job to change his perspective. Instead of making himself the center of the universe, Job should try to see things from God's perspective. Then Job might see that his own concept of justice is faulty and narrow because it is based on the law of retribution.

The first part (38:4–38) of the first speech presents a series of beautiful word-pictures about various aspects of the cosmos: the earth (38:4–7), the sea (38:8–11), the morning (38:12–15), the netherworld (38:16–18), the place of light and darkness (38:19–21), the weather (38:22–30), the constellations (38:31–33), and the storm (38:34–38). Throughout, the emphasis is on God's sovereign power and governance. For example, whereas in other ancient Near Eastern writings creation is often depicted as a battle between the high god and the powers of chaos symbolized especially by the sea, in Job 38:8–11 creation is portrayed as God imposing order on the sea by shutting it in with doors and treating it as a nurse treats an infant: "I made the clouds its garment, and thick darkness its swaddling band" (38:9).

The second part (38:39–39:30) of the first speech presents more word-pictures of the lion (38:39–41), the mountain goats (39:1–4), the wild ass (39:5–8), the wild ox (39:9–12), the ostrich (39:13–18), the horse (39:19–25), and the hawk and the eagle (39:26–30). The section about the ostrich is not in the Greek version, and takes the form of statements rather than questions. The point is that all these animals are beyond human experience or human control. They live through God's governance of the world. Whereas Job wants to make himself the center of the universe, God is offering Job a survey of how the cosmos looks from God's perspective. When God challenges Job to answer (40:1–5), Job is reduced to silence: "I lay my hand on my mouth" (40:4).

The second speech (40:6–41:34) begins with God reminding Job that this is not a conversation between equals: "Have you an arm like God, and can you thunder with a voice like him?" (40:9) Then God focuses on the land creature Behemoth (40:15–24) and the sea creature Leviathan (41:1–34). On the natural level Behemoth displays the characteristics of a hippopotamus and Leviathan those of a crocodile. On the mythical level they represent the chaos monsters defeated by God in the battle of creation. In the theological outlook of the Book of Job, however, they are creatures of God and under God's control. The point is that whereas God exercises control over these powerful creatures, humans like Job do not.

The description of Behemoth emphasizes its raw power ("Its bones are tubes of bronze, its limbs like bars of iron," 40:18) and ability to elude human control ("Can anyone take it with hooks?" 40:24). And yet Behemoth is only "the first of the great acts of God" (40:19; see Genesis 1:24) and remains subject to God's control ("only its Maker can approach it with the sword," 40:19). Likewise, Leviathan cannot be captured by humans and domesticated by them (41:1–8). Everything about Leviathan inspires terror. It is like a fierce dragon: "Out of its nostrils comes smoke . . . and a flame comes out of its mouth" (41:20–21).

When God challenges Job to answer (42:1–6), Job is again reduced to silence. He first apologizes for his boldness: "I have uttered what I did not understand, things too wonderful for me, which I did not know" (42:3b). Then he adds: "I had heard of you by the hearing of the ear, but now my eye sees you; therefore I despise myself, and repent in dust and ashes" (42:6). Much depends on the interpretation of Job's final comments.

Does Job really "repent" in the sense of admitting his sin? The traditional English translations of Job 42:6 may be misleading. The Hebrew verb is *niham* ("be sorry, relent, be comforted") rather than the usual word for "repent" (*shub*). For Job to confess his sin at this point in the conversation seems peculiar. Rather, he appears to be apologizing for his boldness and relenting from his aggressive pursuit of an answer from God.

How then are we to interpret Job's submissions to God in 42:3 and 6? We have only words on a page, and so it is difficult to discern the tone of Job's response to God. One recent approach is to understand them sarcastically—as expressions of Job's cynical disappointment at God's failure to explain to him the real reason for his suffering. A more traditional and likely approach is to find in Job's words his recognition of the mystery of suffering and a real change in his perspective. A related approach sees in Job's responses a profound personal transformation as the result of working through his suffering from God's perspective.

A combination of the second and third interpretations seems most satisfying. Job has gotten the point of God's speeches. Instead of continuing to impose on God his own narrow human concept of justice, Job now looks at the world and at his own life from God's perspective. He has come to see that divine justice cannot be measured by the narrow criteria of human justice.

EPILOGUE (42:7–17): In the first part (42:7–9) of the epilogue God tells Eliphaz that he and his friends were wrong, and that they should offer sacrifice and have Job pray for them. In the second part (42:10–17) God restores Job's fortunes and gives him "twice as much as he had before" (42:10) in family and possessions. Job lives 140 years and dies "old and full of days" (42:17).

This "happy ending" of the book poses another problem of interpretation. A literary explanation is that the prologue and epilogue were originally one narrative that has been split apart by the insertion of the poetic exploration of the mystery of suffering. But the problem remains: The prose narrative seems to affirm what the poetic parts deny—that Job is rewarded for patiently accepting and enduring his sufferings. One could argue that the happy ending ruins the case against the law of retribution that has been so carefully built up in the poetic parts. Other interpreters, however, contend that the restoration of Job and his fortunes is indeed important on the grounds that suffering should not have the final word in the book and that Job should not be left in suffering. God can and does overcome suffering.

Possibilities and Problems

The Book of Job does not solve the problem of innocent suffering. It does, however, establish the inadequacy of those approaches to suffering that place all the responsibility on the person who suffers: the law of retribution, the assumption that all humans are sinful and so deserve to suffer, and the idea that suffering is a discipline from God. There is, of course, some truth to all these approaches. But in some cases of innocent suffering (like Job's), they do not seem to apply.

The Book of Job also shows the inadequacy of imposing a human legal framework on God's role in human suffering. While defending his own innocence and the omnipotence of God, Job comes to recognize that divine justice cannot be measured by human justice, that his relationship is not one between equals, and that the lawsuit mentality fails when applied to understanding his own suffering. It also challenges readers to a spiritual transformation as they try to look at life from God's perspective rather than their own.

For all its literary beauty and theological depth, the Book of Job poses its own set of problems. The interpretative problems connected with chapter 42—whether Job repents, the tone of his submission, and the role of the "happy ending"—mean that the entire book is ambiguous and open to different readings. Of course, most great literature is ambiguous, and much of its greatness lies in its ability to evoke different readings.

The book's depiction of God also raises questions. The God of the speeches from the whirlwind in chapters 38–41 is the majestic Lord of all creation. But rather than supplying real answers to Job's questions, it may seem that God overwhelms Job with his own rhetorical questions and bullies Job into submission. Even more serious is the curious portrayal of God in the prologue. There God enters into a kind of wager with Satan about his servant Job's ability to maintain his righteousness when deprived of his family and possessions and of his health. Does God gamble with human lives? Does God play games with us? Admittedly, the Book of Job is only literature, and the prologue serves to set the scene for the theological debate about the mystery of suffering. Nevertheless, its less than flattering portrayal of God does raise serious theological questions.

From the perspective of Christian theology, the Book of Job is incomplete in its approach to the mystery of suffering. While Satan is prominent in the prologue as a member of the heavenly court, he disappears quickly. And so little or no attention is given to the problem of evil. Also, there is at best a very shadowy concept of afterlife ("Sheol"), and even that is dismissed as a false hope. And no one raises the idea of vicarious or expiatory suffering for others—a concept of great significance not only for the New Testament writers but also for the Servant passages in Isaiah 40–55.

Questions for Reflection, Discussion, and Prayer

1. What are the various explanations that Job's friends put forward as reasons for his suffering? Is there ever any truth in them? Is there any truth in them in Job's case?

2. How do you assess the character of Job as it emerges from the various parts of the book? What is attractive? What is unattractive?

3. What is the point of God's speeches from the whirlwind in chapters 38–41? What effect do they have on you?

4. How do you understand Job's submission in 42:1–6? Is it cynicism, resignation, or mystical transformation?

5. Does the "happy ending" in 42:7–17 spoil the book—or is it salutary and even necessary?

Chapter Four

Suffering and Sacrifice

*If I ever doubted that God once
designated us as the chosen people, I
would believe now that our tribulations
have made us the chosen one.*
                              —Yossel Rakover

M OST PEOPLE—religious people especially—want to
make sense out of their own suffering and the suffer
ings of other people they love or admire. Job's chief
problem was that in his construction of reality it made no sense
that he should be suffering. Job wanted an answer to his question, Why?

One very common way of imbuing suffering with sense is
with the help of the concept of sacrifice. When firefighters die
in the line of duty, it is often said that "they did not die in vain."
When soldiers are killed in battle, we extol their courage and
sacrifice on behalf of their country. Perhaps the most memorable expression of this sentiment is Jesus' saying in John 15:13:
"No one has greater love than this, to lay down one's life for
one's friends."

The concept of sacrifice as a way of making sense out of suffering and death is prominent in the Bible. For most of us today, however, sacrifice is just a metaphor, a figure of speech that we use to describe heroic behavior on behalf of others. For people in biblical times—Jews and Gentiles alike—sacrifice was part of their actual experience. People offered animals, first fruits of crops, wine, and other material goods at shrines and temples. They believed that in doing so they were strengthening their communion with God and expiating or atoning for their sins. In the case of animal sacrifices, blood was an important element. But for people in antiquity, blood was a symbol of life and purification, not a sign of death and disorder. Most of us find all this hard to understand or to have much sympathy for it.

To understand the metaphor of suffering as sacrifice, however, we need to look first at the reality behind it. So this chapter begins with a sketch of sacrifice in the Old Testament. Next it discusses the figure of the Servant of God in Isaiah 40–55, whose suffering is said to have had sacrificial significance for the community of Jewish exiles in Babylon in the sixth century B.C. Then it considers how the early Christians interpreted the suffering of Jesus in the light of what was said about the Suffering Servant in the Old Testament. Next it shows how the early Christians understood Jesus' suffering and death as a sacrifice "for us" and "for our sins," how we might participate in Jesus' suffering and death, why Jesus' suffering is in one sense the "end" of sacrifice, and what happened to the language of sacrifice in the New Testament.

The approach to suffering as sacrifice has been particularly influential in Catholic piety. It underlies that familiar piece of advice to those who suffer, "Offer it up." It appears in various forms of the Sacred Heart and related devotions where one makes "reparation" for the sins of others by prayer and good works. At the beginning of Lent Catholics are urged to embark on a program of Lenten sacrifices. Appeals for money are often accompanied by a call to make sacrifices for the good of this or that cause. And generations of holy Christian people have heroically endured terrible sufferings because they believed that their physical or mental sufferings could function as a sacrifice for the good of others. What then are the biblical foundations of this approach to suffering?

Sacrifice in the Old Testament

Sacrifice was an important part of Old Testament religion, as it has been and is in many other religions. There are several reasons why humans offer sacrifice: to give a gift to God, to initiate or confirm their communion with God, or to make atonement or expiation for their sins.

While the Historical Books of the Old Testament provide evidence that sacrifices were offered to the God of Israel at various places, these same books also describe the movement toward centralizing all sacrifices at the Jerusalem temple. The Pentateuch, especially in its Priestly and Deuteronomistic sections, contains many rules and regulations as to what and how sacrifices were to be offered at the central (and only official) sanctuary in Jerusalem.

The Old Testament describes several kinds of sacrifices: holocausts (where the animal is entirely burnt up), communion sacrifices (accompanying thanksgivings, vows, etc.), offerings of incense or cereal, and expiatory sacrifices (to atone for sins and make reparation to God). The purpose of the expiatory sacrifices was to reestablish the covenant relationship with God when it had been broken through the sins of individuals or of the whole people.

The most important sacrificial rite of expiation took place on the Day of Atonement (see Leviticus 16, 23:27–32; Numbers 29:7–11). On this day the high priest entered the Holy of Holies at the temple and sprinkled blood on and before God's "mercy seat." The use of (animal) blood was essential, since "the life of the flesh is in the blood . . . it is the blood that makes atonement" (Leviticus 17:11). In this culture (and many others) blood symbolizes life (not death) and is regarded as having a purifying or cleansing effect. The reason this rite was carried out every year was to wipe away "the uncleanness of the people of Israel . . . their transgressions, all their sins" (Leviticus 16:16). A prominent feature of the Day of Atonement ritual was the "scapegoat," the goat presented alive before the Lord "to make atonement" and then "sent away into the wilderness of Azazel" (Leviticus 16:10).

Sacrifice was an important part of Old Testament religion. Its theological significance lay in the areas of gift, communion, and expiation or atonement. Most people today, however, find sacrifice hard to understand. It can sound like magic at best or satisfying the desires and demands of an evil or selfish deity at worst. Nevertheless, only with the help of these basic concepts of sacrifice can we understand two biblical figures whose suffering is interpreted in terms of vicarious and expiatory sacrifice: the Servant of God in Isaiah 40–55, and Jesus Christ in the New Testament. Their experiences of suffering presupposed and redefined the biblical concepts of sacrifice.

The Suffering Servant

It has become customary to refer to Isaiah 40–55 as "Second Isaiah" and to Isaiah 56–66 as "Third Isaiah." Whereas Isaiah 1–39, for the most part, presumes a historical setting in the eighth century B.C., the historical setting of Second Isaiah is around 539–537 B.C., when the Persian king Cyrus was conquering Babylon and allowing the exiled Jewish leaders to return to Jerusalem. Third Isaiah was written around 500 B.C., when the exiles had already returned.

The place of Second Isaiah's composition was Babylon, within the exiled Jewish community there. The purpose of Isaiah 40–55 was to encourage the exiles to return and renew Jerusalem. This was no easy task, since some Jews had settled into a stable and even relatively happy existence there. The author used hymns and prophetic speeches to celebrate God as the redeemer of Israel and to evoke enthusiasm for building the New Jerusalem. He portrays the return from exile as a new exodus and a new creation.

One obvious question that the author of Isaiah 40–55 had to face was, How could the God of Israel have allowed the destruction of Jerusalem in 587 B.C. and the exile of its political and religious leadership? In answering this question, he agreed with the Deuteronomist(s) and the pre-exilic prophets that these events were punishments for Israel's sins. But his work begins with the proclamation that the time of Israel's punishments is over: "her penalty is paid; . . . she has received from the LORD's hand double for all her sins" (Isaiah 40:2).

The real contribution of Second Isaiah to the biblical theme of suffering, however, lies in introducing the theme of vicarious (for others) and expiatory (atoning for sins) suffering. This theme is developed especially with reference to the figure of the Suffering Servant in Isaiah 52:13–53:12. That passage contends that the suffering of God's Servant had a purpose and a positive effect for others. His suffering wiped away the sins of God's people and so made it possible for them to join in the new exodus and to build the New Jerusalem.

There are four passages in Second Isaiah that refer to God's Servant: 42:1–9; 49:1–13; 50:4–11; and 52:13–53:12. Whether these four poems form a literary unit or ever existed outside their present literary context in Isaiah 40–55 are matters of ongoing dispute among scholars. While the first two passages say little or nothing about the Servant's suffering, the latter two texts develop the theme in detail.

The first Servant song (42:1–9) focuses on God's choice of the Servant ("my servant whom I uphold, my chosen"), his gentle and nonviolent character ("a bruised reed he will not break"), and his mission to establish "justice in the earth" and to serve as "a light to the nations."

The second Servant song (49:1–13) begins with the Servant describing his call from God and identifying himself as

Israel: "And he [God] said to me, 'You are my servant, Israel, in whom I will be glorified'" (49:3). But then when God speaks in 49:5–13, the Servant is said to have a mission on Israel's behalf: "to bring Jacob back to him, and that Israel might be gathered to him" (49:5). The Servant is to be "a light to the nations" (49:6) and is given the task to join in the return to Jerusalem as a new exodus. The only note of suffering is the Servant's protestation about his own exhaustion and frustration ("I have labored in vain, I have spent my strength for nothing and vanity," 49:4). But these gloomy thoughts are quickly wiped away by his assertion that "my cause is with the LORD, and my reward with my God" (49:4).

Who is this Servant of God? There is surely a close connection with Israel. Almost everything said about the Servant is also said about Israel in Second Isaiah. But there are some significant differences. For example, whereas Israel is rebellious and sinful (Isaiah 48:4), the Servant is faithful and not rebellious (50:5, 53:4–6, 12). And yet the Servant has a mission vis-à-vis Israel (see 49:4–5) and so is not simply the same as Israel.

The collective interpretations identify the Servant as all Israel or a group within Israel (the exiled community as a whole, a prophetic school within the exiled community, or some other group). The individual interpretations include the legitimate claimant to the high priesthood or the kingship of Judah, some leader of the exiled community, a prophet, the author himself, or Moses. Early Christians, of course, identified Jesus as the Servant of God.

The third Servant song (50:4–11) contains a graphic description of his suffering: "I gave my back to those who struck me, and my cheeks to those who pulled out my beard; I did not hide my face from insult and spitting" (50:6). But the Servant is still confident that God is on his side, and so he claims that he was not disgraced in the past and that he is confident that he will not be shamed in the future: "It is the Lord GOD who helps me; who will declare me guilty?" (50:9) Nothing yet has been said about the purpose and value of the Servant's suffering.

The fourth Servant song (52:13–53:12) provides the most extensive treatment of the Servant's suffering. The general structure of this very important text is clear from the changes in the speaker: God (52:13–15), "we"(53:1–10), and God (53:11–12).

In God's first statement (52:13–15) the emphasis is on the astonishing transformation that "my servant" has undergone. Whereas previously the Servant's appearance was marked "beyond human semblance," now God proclaims that his Servant will prosper and "be exalted and lifted up."

In the central section (53:1–10) the human speakers ("we") in 53:1–3 express their own surprise at the transformation of God's Servant. They observe that there was nothing exceptional or attractive about the Servant. They go on to describe the Servant as "despised and rejected by others; a man of suffering and acquainted with infirmity" (53:3). The speakers ("we") probably represent the exiled Jewish community in Babylon. The identity of the Servant remains mysterious, but one gets the impression of an individual whose suffering has significance for the whole people.

The theme of his vicarious and expiatory suffering is developed in 53:4–6. That the Servant suffered for others is expressed in several ways: "Surely he has borne our infirmities and carried our diseases . . . he was wounded for our transgressions, crushed for our iniquities." That the Servant's suffering had positive consequences for others is also emphasized: "upon him was the punishment that made us whole, and by his bruises we are healed." It is as if all the punishments due to all the sins of God's people have been visited upon the figure of God's Servant: "the LORD has laid on him the iniquity of us all." And the result of the Servant's suffering is the healing and the wholeness of God's people. In the background is the logic of sacrifice as a means of atoning for sin and renewing the relationship with God. With the Jerusalem temple destroyed, it was not possible for Jews to offer material sacrifices, and so the suffering of God's Servant does what material sacrifices could not do. It brings about right relationship with God and makes it possible for the exiled community to return to its Holy City.

Entirely innocent, the Servant, according to 53:7–9, suffered unjustly. When oppressed and afflicted, he suffered in silence and was "like a lamb that is led to the slaughter." He was taken away "by a perversion of justice" and was either put to death or came very close to death: "they made his grave with the wicked." Whether he died and was buried in that grave is not clear. What is clear is the innocence of God's Servant ("no violence . . . no deceit") and the vicarious and expiatory character of his suffering ("stricken for the transgression of my people").

That the Servant did not actually die is suggested by 53:10: "he shall see his offspring, and shall prolong his days." In any case, the Servant is rewarded for his pain and suffering. His suffering is interpreted as part of God's plan rather than as a sign of God's displeasure toward him personally: "it was the will of the LORD to crush him with pain." And again the Servant's suffering is understood in terms of the logic of sacrifice: "you make his life an offering for sin."

When God speaks again, in 53:11–12, he reaffirms the identity of this suffering figure as "the righteous one, my servant." God also reaffirms the vicarious and expiatory character of the Servant's suffering: "he shall bear their iniquities . . . he bore the sin of many, and made intercession for the transgressors." Although the Servant suffered (or almost underwent) a shameful death, the result of his suffering is not only personal vindication but also justification for others: "the righteous one, my servant, shall make many righteous."

In the historical context of Israel's exile in Babylon in the sixth century B.C., the figure of the Servant (whoever he may have been) helped to explain why the suffering of the Exile happened (because of Israel's sins) and why it was now over (because through the Servant's vicarious and expiatory suffering Israel had "paid double" for its sins, see Isaiah 40:2). The Servant's suffering was the effective sacrifice for the people's sins and made possible its renewed relationship with God.

Comparison with the Book of Job can highlight the distinctive contributions of the Suffering Servant figure to the biblical understanding of suffering. Whereas the Book of Job is set long ago and far away and so is essentially timeless (whatever its actual historical origin may have been), the Servant passages reflect the experiences of historic Israel in exile at Babylon around 539–537 B.C. Whereas the Book of Job is concerned with the sufferings of one righteous man (whatever Job's representative significance may be), the Servant passages concern the sufferings of someone whose identity resides especially in his representative significance. Whereas the Book of Job deals with the apparent meaninglessness of Job's suffering, the Servant passages imbue with meaning not only the sufferings of the Servant but also the sufferings of Israel in exile. The Servant's sufferings have made reparation for the people's sins and have made possible what seems to be a new exodus and a new creation for God's people.

Jesus as the Servant of God

At various points the Gospels bear witness to the early Christian identification of Jesus as the Servant of God. The elderly Simeon prophesies that the child Jesus will be a "light to the nations" (Luke 2:32; see Isaiah 42:6, 49:6). At his baptism by John, Jesus is identified by the heavenly voice as "my Son, the Beloved; with you I am well pleased" (Mark 1:11; see Isaiah 42:1). John the Baptist describes Jesus as "the Lamb of God who takes away the sin of the world" (John 1:29; see Isaiah 53:7, 12). Matthew interprets Jesus' healing activities with the help of Isaiah 53:4: "He took our infirmities and bore our diseases" (Matthew 8:17). And Matthew quotes Isaiah 42:1–4 in full, in 12:18–21, to shed light on Jesus' ministry and the mixed reception he received. At the transfiguration the heavenly voice again identifies Jesus as "my Son, the beloved" (Mark 9:7). In Mark 10:45 Jesus proclaims that he has come "to give his life as a ransom for many" (see Isaiah 53:10). At his death on the cross Jesus is said to have been "counted among the lawless" (Luke 22:37; see Isaiah 53:9).

The story of Philip and the Ethiopian eunuch (probably a Jew or a proselyte) in Acts 8:26–40 revolves around the proper interpretation of Isaiah 53:7–8: "Like a sheep he was led to the slaughter. . . ." When the Ethiopian wants to know about whom the prophet was speaking, Philip shares with him the good news about Jesus and urges him to be baptized. For Philip and the Ethiopian, Jesus as the Servant of God is the key to understanding all the Scriptures of Israel. First Peter 2:22 recommends to suffering Christians that they follow the example of the innocent and gentle Jesus with a quotation of Isaiah 53:9: "He committed no sin, and no deceit was found in his mouth."

These and other New Testament texts affirm that Jesus was the Servant of God, and call upon the relevant passages in Second Isaiah to help explain how the beloved Son of God could have suffered and died a cruel death. The early Christians also found in the fourth Servant song (Isaiah 52:13–53:12) the basis for interpreting Jesus' suffering and death as a sacrifice for sins.

Jesus' Suffering and Death as a Sacrifice

Paul's letters, written between A.D. 51 and 58, are the earliest complete documents in the New Testament. At many points in them, Paul writes in such a way that he is clearly quoting even earlier expressions of Christian faith. Many of these credal formulas refer to Jesus' death as being "for us" and "for our sins"— as a vicarious and expiatory sacrifice. In recounting Jesus' words over the bread at the Last Supper, Paul in 1 Corinthians 11:24 writes, "This is my body that is for you." When quoting the tradition about Jesus' death and resurrection that he had received and now hands on to the Corinthians, Paul, in 1 Corinthians 15:3, states that "Christ died for our sins." And in Romans 3:25 he describes Jesus as the one "whom God put forward as a sacrifice of atonement by his blood." These pre-Pauline formulas interpret Jesus' death as a sacrifice for sins. So in the twenty or twenty-five years between Jesus' death and the earliest letters in the New Testament, there was already a lively tradition that explained Jesus' death in terms of a sacrifice for sins.

Paul made this sacrificial interpretation of Jesus' suffering his own. When writing to the Galatians, he describes Jesus as the one "who gave himself for our sins to set us free from the present evil age" (1:4). In his argument about life under the Law, Paul affirms that "Christ redeemed us from the curse of the law by becoming a curse for us" (Galatians 3:13). In 2 Corinthians Paul says that "one died for all" (5:14) and that "for our sake" God "made him to be sin who knew no sin" (5:21). In other words, Jesus' suffering and death constituted the truly effective "sin offering" that made possible right relationship with God (justification). In Romans Paul states that "at the right time Christ died for the ungodly" (5:6) and reminds his readers that they should regard all their fellow Christians as "one for whom Christ died" (14:15). These and other Pauline texts assert that Jesus suffered and died as God's Servant on our behalf ("for us" and "for our sins") and so has made available to all peoples— Jews and Gentiles alike— the benefits of his death and resurrection (access to God, sanctification, and so on). The earliest Christians interpreted Jesus' death as a sacrifice for sins.

Another basic theme of Paul's theology is Christian life as sharing in and identifying with Jesus' death and resurrection. According to Philippians 3:10, Paul's prayer is "that I may share his sufferings, becoming like him in his death, that if possible I may attain the resurrection from death." In 2 Corinthians 1:3–7, Paul presents this sharing and identification as a possibility for all Christians: "as we share abundantly in Christ's sufferings, so through Christ we share abundantly in comfort too." And in 2 Corinthians 4:10 Paul describes Christian life as "always carrying in the body the death of Jesus, so that the life of Jesus may also be manifested in our bodies." If it is proper to speak of mysticism with reference to Paul's theology, it is the mysticism of identification with Jesus' suffering and death: "I have been cru-cified with Christ; and it is no longer I who live, but it is Christ who lives in me" (Galatians 2:19–20).

In the context of a discussion about Jesus' death as a sac-rifice and about Christian participation in it, the statement attributed to Paul in Colossians 1:24 demands special attention because it is open to theological misunderstanding: "I am now rejoicing in my sufferings for your sake, and in my flesh I am completing what is lacking in Christ's afflictions for the sake of his body, that is, the church." Many scholars today regard the letter to the Colossians as having been composed in Paul's name by a disciple or an admirer of Paul after his death. It represents what Paul would have said in addressing a situation in western Asia Minor (present-day Turkey) around A.D. 80.

Echoing Paul's own statements in his undisputed letters, this text first asserts that Paul suffers on behalf of other Chris-tians and rejoices to do so. The second part of the text affirms that Paul is "completing what is lacking in Christ's afflictions." The key word here is "afflictions." This is not the usual word for referring to sufferings of Christ. Moreover, the verse cannot mean that there was something deficient or inadequate about the sufferings of Christ that they need to be completed some-how. In fact, the whole thrust of the letter to the Colossians (and the other books of the New Testament) is to insist on the perfect sufficiency of Christ's sufferings: "For in him all the full-ness of God was pleased to dwell, and through him God was pleased to reconcile to himself all things, whether on earth or in heaven, by making peace through the blood of his cross" (Colossians 1:19–20).

What then are the "afflictions" of Christ? According to Jewish texts from around the time of the New Testament (see 1 Enoch 47:1–4; 2 Baruch 30:2), the "afflictions" (or "woes" or "birthpangs") of the Messiah refer to the fixed amount or quota of sufferings set by God before the Messiah and the fullness of God's kingdom can come. So in Colossians 1:24 the sufferings of Paul the apostle are being credited to this account, as it were.

A similar motif appears in Mark 13:20, where it said that God "for the sake of the elect . . . has cut short those days." Read against its Jewish and early Christian background, Colossians 1:24 concerns filling up the "afflictions" of the Messiah, not the insufficiency of Christ's suffering and death.

The most sustained New Testament reflection on the perfect sufficiency of Christ's suffering appears in what is called the Letter to the Hebrews. In fact, this work is a long sermon intended for Jewish Christians who had become discouraged in their new faith and were tempted to revert to Judaism. The author (certainly not Paul) insists that Christ is both the perfect sacrifice, because his death really took away sins, and the genuine high priest, because he offered himself willingly. His perfect sacrifice has rendered obsolete and otiose the sacrifices of the Jewish high priests: "Unlike the other high priests, he [Christ] has no need to offer sacrifices day after day, first for his own sins, and then for those of his people; this he did once for all when he offered himself" (Hebrews 7:27). Jesus' willing embrace of his death on the cross represents the perfect sacrifice for sins ("once for all"). There is no reason for other sacrifices, since "we have been sanctified through the offering of the body of Jesus Christ once for all" (10:10). His "single sacrifice" (10:12) was perfectly sufficient.

Was the conviction that Christ's perfect sacrifice meant the end of all other material sacrifices a natural theological development? Or was it influenced by the destruction of the Jerusalem temple in A.D. 70 and the cessation of sacrifices there? This is a matter of debate among biblical scholars. In either case, the author of Hebrews (and other early Christian writers) goes on to use the terminology of "sacrifice" in a more spiritual sense. Toward the end of his sermon, he exhorts his audience in this way: "let us continually offer a sacrifice of praise to God, that is, the fruit of lips that confess his name" (13:15). The perfectly sufficient sacrifice offered by Christ the high priest marks the end of material sacrifices for Christians. And so Christians begin to apply the language of sacrifice to their own worship and their good deeds. This development can be seen already in Paul's letter to the Romans when he exhorts Christians "to present your bodies as a living sacrifice, holy and acceptable to God, which is your spiritual worship" (12:1).

Possibilities and Problems

On a purely human level, understanding suffering as a sacrifice for the good of others expresses a noble and heroic ideal. At the same time, it can and does imbue suffering with meaning and significance, and so can help to alleviate the effects of suffering.

On the level of Christian theology, the sacrificial interpretation of suffering is very important. It is central to the New Testament's understanding of Jesus' passion and death and to its conception of Christian life as a whole. When Christians suffer they can and do share in Jesus' sufferings. And their sufferings, while they cannot complete the suffering of Christ (because Christ's sacrifice is already perfect and sufficient for salvation), can at least have an effect on the "afflictions" of the Messiah (see Colossians 1:24) and so facilitate the full coming of God's kingdom. Our sufferings are linked to the paschal mystery of Jesus' passion, death, and resurrection, and have cosmic significance.

Despite the many positive contributions of understanding suffering as sacrifice, this approach also presents some problems for people today. Because few Western people have firsthand experiences of material sacrifice today, we find it hard to grasp. When I speak about sacrifice in the Bible to Americans or Europeans today, I get mainly blank stares. But when I talk with African or Asian students, whose traditional religions still practice sacrifice, they understand the biblical concepts right away.

Also the slogan "Offer it up" frequently sets off alarms in the minds and hearts of many people today. It has too often been used as an excuse for people in religious or political power to impose their wills on suffering people. Many women especially feel that this approach has been imposed on them as an ideal and then used as a means of dominating or manipulating them. Where many men talk about heroic self-sacrifice, many women see the same old patriarchalism being imposed on them. In discussions about sacrifice and suffering, I have found that men embrace the idea quickly while many women today have serious reservations about its applications to specific cases of suffering.

Jews are also cautious about interpreting suffering in sacrificial terms. Perhaps out of reaction to the early Christians' usurpation of the Suffering Servant figure and the application of it to the suffering of Jesus, the Jewish tradition seldom uses the Servant songs in Second Isaiah to illumine individual cases of suffering. Rather, a collective interpretation where the Servant stands for Israel is much favored. Also, among Jews today there is growing resistance to the term *Holocaust* to describe the murder of six million Jews under the Nazis. The problem is that "Holocaust" is a religious word ("whole burnt offering") that could imply a sacrificial interpretation. Not everyone wants to interpret Hitler's war against the Jews in this framework. And so there is growing sentiment for using the Hebrew word *Shoah*, which simply means "destruction" or "devastation" and is not so tied to a theological perspective.

In the history of Christian theology the sacrificial understanding of Jesus' suffering and death has led to some peculiar ideas. Saint Anselm, a twelfth-century British monk and an archbishop of Canterbury, developed what is called the *substitution theory of atonement.* Anselm understood sin as taking honor from God and as remitted only by punishment to make satisfaction or reparation. To answer the question why God became human in Christ, Anselm reasoned that the honor of God besmirched by human sin could be restored only by one who was both human (but not a sinner) and divine. By becoming human Christ was able to repay the debt owed to God by humans. The problem is that Anselm has taken some biblical ideas and pushed them far beyond what the Bible does with them.

Another peculiar idea is the persistent belief that we can add to the sacrifice of Christ. We can share in Christ's sufferings, and we can fill up the "afflictions" of the Messiah. But according to the New Testament, the sacrifice of Christ was perfect and sufficient, and there was nothing lacking in his sufferings.

Questions for Reflection, Discussion, and Prayer

1. How would you explain the logic of sacrifice? Is this concept meaningful or helpful to you?

2. What evidence in Isaiah 52:13–53:12 points to the vicarious and expiatory nature of the Servant's suffering?

3. In what sense was Christ's death a sacrifice for our sins?

4. What are the theological consequences of saying that Christ "offered for all time a single sacrifice for sins" (Hebrews 10:12)?

5. How do you assess Anselm's substitution theory of atonement? What theological problems does it raise?

Chapter Five

The Apocalyptic Solution

*It is a time when God has veiled His
countenance from the world, sacrificing
mankind to its wild instincts. . . . What
more must transpire before You unveil
Your countenance again to the world?*
—Yossel Rakover

THE LITERATURE of Jewish apocalypticism is rooted in the problem of suffering. From a historical perspective it arose out of the conflict between God's promises to Israel and Israel's political subjugation to a series of foreign empires: Babylonians, Persians, Greeks, Ptolemies, Seleucids, and Romans. Whether Jewish apocalypticism was a natural development of ancient Israel's traditions or influenced by foreign (especially Persian) ideas is a matter of long-standing debate among scholars. It is clear, however, as the Book of Daniel shows, that apocalyptic is the literature of dispossessed and oppressed people. According to the apocalyptic perspective, only a divine intervention could rescue God's people from their present distress and bring about a correspondence between God's promises to the chosen people and the present historical situation of that people.

The Jewish apocalyptic solution to the problem of suffering made it possible to maintain the three propositions of theodicy: God is omnipotent; God is just; and the righteous are rewarded and the wicked are punished. The principle of retribution remains in force—but its execution is not in the present time. When God's kingdom comes, then the righteous will be vindicated and the wicked will be punished or annihilated. This approach preserves the justice of God by deferring rewards and punishments to the last judgment or to some other divine intervention. It also preserves the sovereignty of God by attributing the present good fortune of the wicked and the suffering of the righteous to the mysterious plan of God or to an evil force now active in history but under the ultimate control of God. The apocalyptic solution encourages suffering people to persist in their righteousness, to trust in the promise of God, and to hope that God will unveil his countenance to the world.

The Book of Daniel

The Book of Daniel was composed around 165 B.C. to respond to a very specific crisis in the land of Israel: the substitution of a pagan cult for the worship of the God of Israel in the Jerusalem temple. This development raised important theological questions for some within the Jewish people: How could God allow this to happen? Why were good and righteous Jews suffering for trying to remain faithful to God's covenant? Why were the evildoers appearing to triumph over the righteous?

This crisis had a background in Greek and Near Eastern history. By the time of the death of Alexander the Great in 323 B.C., the land of Israel along with neighboring lands had become part of Alexander's Hellenistic empire. From Alexander's death to 200 B.C. Judea was administered by the Egyptian or Ptolemaic branch of Alexander's successors. But around 200 B.C. Judea became subject to the Syrian or Seleucid branch. At first the Judeans were allowed to observe their traditional rituals, laws, and customs. With the accession of Antiochus IV Epiphanes to the Seleucid throne in 175 B.C., there was a change in policy toward Judea.

There is a long-standing debate about Antiochus's precise motives and about the extent to which he received encouragement and support from some within the local Judean community (see 1 Maccabees 1:11–15). Whatever the historical motives and responsibilities may have been, the ancient Jewish sources present the people's suffering as the result of a decree from Antiochus prohibiting the observance of the Torah as the law for Jews and his establishment of the cult of "the Most High God" in the Jerusalem temple (see 1 Maccabees 1:41–61). From the perspective of some in Judea (including the circle behind the Book of Daniel), the pagan cult amounted to "a desolating sacrilege" or, as it is traditionally rendered, "the abomination of desolation."

The crisis was resolved to some extent when Judas Maccabeus and his supporters captured the temple area in 164 B.C. and restored the traditional worship of the God of Israel. This resolution seems to have occurred after the composition of the Book of Daniel, and so it appears that it was composed around 165 B.C. Rather than expecting the Maccabees to solve the problem, the author of the Book of Daniel looked forward to the coming of God's kingdom—a more direct divine intervention and a more definitive resolution in favor of those in Israel who had remained faithful to God's covenant.

While the Book of Daniel was composed in Judea around 165 B.C., the stories and visions that constitute it are set in the courts of the Babylonian and Persian kings of the sixth century B.C. Daniel, along with his companions, appears as a Jewish courtier who issues prophecies about the course of world history from the sixth century to the second century B.C. Some of the traditions in the book may well antedate its composition around 165 B.C. Nevertheless, almost everything in the book has been adapted to illumine the crisis precipitated by Antiochus and his Jewish collaborators.

The text appears in two languages. Chapters 1 and 8–12 are in Hebrew, while chapters 2–7 are in Aramaic. The first six chapters are stories about Daniel in the form of conflicts and contests that are presented in the third person ("he"). The last six chapters are visions that Daniel narrates in the first person ("I"). The book emerged from and spoke to a Jewish group that in this crisis looked for deliverance from God alone.

It is customary to classify the Book of Daniel as an apocalypse. The word *apocalypse* derives from the Greek term for "revelation." Apocalypses present revelations about the future or about the heavenly realm. Since these topics transcend ordinary human knowledge, there is need for special revelations from God about them. Since many parts of the book convey revelations about the future and about the heavenly court, it is appropriate to classify the whole book as an apocalypse.

The word "apocalyptic" is often used to describe the kind of thinking that is found in apocalypses, and so it is appropriate to describe the approach to the problem of suffering in the Book of Daniel as the apocalyptic solution.

The book was composed to address the suffering among God's people in Judea around 165 B.C. The central institutions of biblical Israel—the Torah, the Temple, and the Land—were now all in the wrong hands. And faithful Jews were suffering, even to the point of death. The apocalyptic solution holds together the suffering of righteous Jews, the omnipotence of God, and the justice of God. It does so by deferring the full display of God's power and justice to the future (the kingdom of God). This (imminent) display of God's rule will mark the vindication of the suffering righteous ones and the punishment of their evil opponents. That God will remain faithful to his promises is certain. In the meantime, the message of the Book of Daniel is to hold firm in fidelity since the suffering is only temporary.

CONFLICTS AND CONTESTS (1–6): The first six chapters are stories about Daniel and his fellow Jewish courtiers. There are conflicts about food (chap. 1), worship (chap. 3), and prayer (chap. 6).

There are contests about interpreting the king's dreams (chaps. 2 and 4) and the handwriting on the wall (chap. 5). While set in the courts of sixth-century B.C. Babylonian and Persian kings, these stories spoke eloquently to the Judean situation in the second century B.C. Their message is simple: God is in control of human history; the power of the evildoers and the suffering that they inflict are temporary; and so it is necessary to remain faithful in the present.

The first conflict (chap. 1) concerns whether Daniel and his Jewish companions should partake of "the royal ration of food and wine" (1:5). Convinced that these rations would bring ritual defilement upon them, they propose to live on vegetables and water for ten days. They emerge "better and fatter" (1:15) than the other courtiers. By avoiding the defiling food and drink, the Jewish courtiers not only prospered physically but also received prominent positions at the royal court. The message to Jews in the second century was clear: Remain faithful to Jewish food laws and customs and you will not perish.

The first contest (chap. 2) concerns the interpretation of King Nebuchadnezzar's dream about a great statue with a head of gold, chest and arms of silver, middle and thighs of bronze, legs of iron, and feet partly of iron and partly of clay (2:31–35). With God's help Daniel interprets the various parts as referring to the four kingdoms between the sixth and second centuries: Babylon, Media, Persia, and Greece. The iron/clay feet allude to the divided Greek kingdom (Ptolemies and Seleucids) and to the efforts at strengthening it by marriage alliances. The stone that shatters the statue refers to the kingdom that God will set up to replace these four empires. The message to Jews in the second century was clear: The reign of foreigners over Judea is only temporary and will soon yield to the kingdom of God.

The second conflict (chap. 3) begins with the royal decree that everyone in the Babylonian Empire must fall down to worship a golden statue. The Jewish courtiers refuse to participate on grounds of conscience, and so they are cast into a furnace of blazing fire. They emerge miraculously unharmed and receive promotions at the court. The message to Jews in the second century was clear: Refuse to worship idols and you will not be harmed.

The second contest (chap. 4) concerns the interpretation of King Nebuchadnezzar's dream about the cutting down of a great tree and about a man whose mind became like that of an animal. Daniel recognizes that "the tree that you saw . . . it is you, O king!" (4:20, 22) The motif of the "crazy king" may have been attached originally to the Babylonian king Nabonidus. But it probably also fit rumors about Antiochus's own erratic behavior that won him the nickname "mad man" (*epimanes*). The message to Jews in the second century was clear: The evil king will soon be brought down and so hold firm in the present.

The third contest (chap. 5) concerns the interpretation of the handwriting that mysteriously appears on the wall of the royal banquet hall. Only Daniel recognizes that "MENE, MENE, TEKEL, PARSIN" ("numbered, numbered, weighed, divided") refers to the imminent end of the Babylonian Empire and the transfer of its power to the Medes and Persians (5:24–28). The message to Jews in the second century was clear: The evil empire will end soon and so hold firm in the present.

The third conflict (chap. 6) begins with a royal decree that those who refuse to pray to King Darius alone will be thrown into a pit of lions. For reasons of conscience, Daniel refuses to obey the decree, and so he is cast into the pit. As in chapter 3, Daniel emerges unharmed. There may be hints in this story about Antiochus's own pretensions to divinity. The message to Jews in the second century was clear: Refrain from emperor worship and God will protect you from harm.

Taken together these stories about conflicts and contests spoke to the crisis in Judea in the second century B.C. They affirm the sovereignty of the God of Israel and portray the power of the foreign kings as temporary and subject to the God of Israel. The present sufferings of God's people will soon be ended by the direct intervention of God, and the divine justice will be made manifest. In the meantime remain faithful to the God of Israel and resist the worship of false gods.

THREE VISIONS AND A LAMENT (7–12): In the second half of the book, Daniel narrates in the first-person singular ("I") three visions about the future (chaps. 7, 8, 10–12) and laments over Israel's sinfulness as the cause of the present suffering (chap. 9). He affirms the sovereignty of the God of Israel and promises that God's justice will soon be visible to all.

The first vision (chap. 7) concerns four beasts coming up from the sea. The first three look like a lion (with eagle's wings), a bear, and a leopard, respectively. They symbolize (as in chap. 2) the first three empires: Babylon, Media, and Persia. The fourth beast, who is "terrifying and dreadful and exceedingly strong" (7:7), symbolizes the Hellenistic Empire begun by Alexander the Great. The progeny of the fourth beast is a little horn with "a mouth speaking arrogantly" (7:8)—clearly a reference to Antiochus IV Epiphanes.

The scene shifts to the heavenly court where "an Ancient One" presides over the judgment of the beasts: "The court sat in judgment, and the books were opened" (7:10). The result is the destruction of the last beast (Antiochus) and the end of the power of all the other empires ("their dominion was taken away," 7:12). The vision ends with a transfer of power from the Ancient One to the One like a Human Being: "to him was given dominion and glory and kingship . . . an everlasting dominion that shall not pass away" (7:14).

The interpretation given by Daniel in 7:15–28 generally confirms what is already obvious from the vision. The great exception concerns the identification of the One like a Human Being. Whereas one might suppose this figure to be an angel (most likely Michael), in the interpretation he is identified collectively as "the holy ones of the Most High" (7:18, 27). Whether "the holy ones" are angels, members of a Jewish sect, a mixture of the two, or "all Israel" understood collectively is a matter of long-standing exegetical dispute.

Behind the vision and its interpretation is the conviction that the God of Israel is the real ruler and that the power of the four great empires is temporary and subject to this God's direction. This God will exact punishment from the wicked King Antiochus and will give everlasting power to "the holy ones of the Most High" who represent the people of God. Nothing is said in chapter 7 about any wrongdoing on Israel's part. Rather, the elevation of the holy ones is presented as the natural outcome of God's plan.

The second vision (chap. 8) follows the pattern of vision and interpretation. In the third year of the Babylonian king Belshazzar's reign, Daniel is granted a vision of a ram with two horns (the empires of the Medes and the Persians) and of a male goat "from the west" (Alexander). The male goat easily defeats the ram. But "at the height of its power the great horn was broken" (8:8)—clearly a reference to Alexander's early death. In its place (see 8:8–9) there came up "four prominent horns" (Alexander's successors), and out of them came "another horn, a little one" (Antiochus). As in chapters 2 and 7, the course of world history is portrayed in terms of the "four empire" schema. This schema antedated the Book of Daniel, a fact supported by the artificiality of its imposition in this book (which has to make the Medes and Persians into two successive and separate empires).

The arrogance of the little horn (Antiochus) reaches its height in his taking away the daily sacrifice from the Jerusalem temple and "overturning the sanctuary." But Antiochus's triumph is only temporary; that is, for 2,300 evenings and mornings = 1,150 days = three and a half years (see 8:14).

Again the interpretation (8:15–27) generally confirms what is obvious from the vision. There are, however, three elements that contribute to the distinctively apocalyptic approach to suffering. The emphasis on the "end" (8:17, 19) suggests a definitive change in the course of world history. Also there is, in 8:23, the idea of the end of the dominion of the four empires as coinciding with the time "when the transgressions have reached their full measure" in the rise of the arrogant King Antiochus. Finally, his power will be broken "not by human hands" (8:25); that is, it will be broken by God's hand. The motifs of the end-time, the full measure or quota of transgressions, and divine agency in bringing about the new kingdom become part of the apocalyptic solution to the present sufferings of God's faithful people. The power and justice of the God of Israel will be made manifest to all creation in God's own time (which is expected to be soon, see 8:14).

Daniel's lament (chap. 9) explains that Israel is suffering as a punishment for its sins. The chapter concludes with a timetable for when the suffering will cease. Whereas the narratives in the first half of the book and the visions in the second half blame the people's distress on the arrogance of foreign kings (all of them pointing toward Antiochus IV), Daniel's lament in 9:4–19 is a communal confession of sins: "we have sinned and done wrong . . . we have rebelled . . . we have disobeyed his voice . . . we have done wickedly." The capture and destruction of Jerusalem in the sixth century (which amounts to recent history in the book's narrative setting) is interpreted (as elsewhere in the Hebrew Bible) as the just punishment for Israel's sins: "because of our sins and the iniquities of our ancestors, Jerusalem and your people have become a disgrace among all our neighbors" (9:16). In the context of the book's composition in the second century B.C., the implication is that the current dire state of Jerusalem and its temple is likewise just punishment for the people's sins. Thus Daniel's lament inserts the law of retribution—present suffering as just punishment for sins—into the framework of the apocalyptic approach. His hope is that God will "let your face shine upon your desolated sanctuary" (9:17). His hope is based not "on the ground of our righteousness, but on the ground of your great mercies" (9:18).

The angel Gabriel assures Daniel that the people will be able "to put an end to sin and to atone for iniquity" (9:24). He goes on to offer a timetable of seventy weeks. After seven weeks (see Jeremiah 25:11, 29:10) the city of Jerusalem will be rebuilt and will remain standing "but in a troubled time" (9:25) for sixty-two weeks—roughly to the time of Antiochus IV. The first half of the one remaining week—roughly the time of the book's composition—will be dominated by "the desolator" (Antiochus IV), who will set up "an abomination that desolates" (9:27). So the time is short. According to this timetable (see 12:7, 11, 12), Israel will soon have atoned for its sins and the power of the arrogant king will soon be broken. Then the power and justice of the God of Israel will be manifest to all creation.

The third vision (chaps. 10–12) presents a survey of history from the sixth century to around 165 B.C. The first phase concerns the Persian kings, Alexander, the Ptolemies and Seleucids, and the Third Syrian War of 246–241 B.C. The angel narrates these events as the unfolding of the divine plan. However, when he comes to Antiochus III (223–187 B.C.), he emphasizes that king's arrogance and insolence. This judgment prepares for the extended portrait of Antiochus IV, in 11:20–39, as one who outdid all his predecessors in arrogance and evildoing.

The description of Antiochus IV's dealings with Judea calls attention to a split among Judeans between those who forsake "the holy covenant" and those who remain faithful to it (11:30; see 1 Maccabees 1:11–15). While the former will be seduced into participating in "the abomination that makes desolate" (11:31), the "wise" shall stand firm even in the face of suffering. The way of active military resistance advocated by the Maccabees seems to be dismissed as at best "a little help" (11:34). Rather, the positive ideal for the "wise" is patient endurance until God's definitive intervention: "Some of the wise shall fall, so that they may be refined, purified, and cleansed, until the time of the end, for there is still an interval until the time appointed" (11:35).

The arrogance of Antiochus IV is highlighted in 11:36–39: "He shall exalt himself and consider himself greater than any god, and shall speak horrendous things against the God of gods" (11:36). He is accused of religious innovation in promoting the cult of "the god of the fortresses" (11:38).

Nevertheless, his apparent triumph is only temporary—"until the period of wrath is completed" (11:36). Despite appearances, the God of Israel is neither powerless nor unjust. Rather, very soon Antiochus IV will be brought down, and the righteous wise will be vindicated (see 12:1–3).

In 11:40–45 the vision proceeds to imagine Antiochus IV as the victim of his own overreaching arrogance: "he shall come to his end, with no one to help him" (11:45; compare 1 Maccabees 6:12–17; 2 Maccabees 1:11–17, 9:1–29). The "wise," however, are to be vindicated after "a time of anguish" (12:1) in which Michael shall act as the protector of God's people. Those who have died before the great tribulation will be awakened from the sleep of death, with the righteous wise ones rising "to everlasting life" and the wicked ones "to shame and everlasting contempt" (12:2). The goal and end of this grand vision of history is the vindication of those within Judea who have remained faithful: "Those who are wise shall shine like the brightness of the sky, and those who lead many to righteousness, like the stars forever and ever" (12:3). The suffering of God's people is only temporary, and their vindication is very near.

How near? The question "How long?" receives several answers in 12:5–12, each expressing confidence in the imminence of the end and each pushing the precise time further into the future. There are three timetables: "a time, two times, and a half a time" (12:7, see 8:14, 9:26–27) = three and a half years; 1,290 days (12:11); and 1,335 days (12:12). The book ends with a promise of resurrection and vindication for Daniel himself: "you shall rise for your reward at the end of the days" (12:12).

The third vision affirms the various aspects of the apocalyptic approach to the mystery of suffering: The God of Israel exercises sovereignty over the course of history; the sufferings of the righteous are only temporary; and at the proper time, God's justice will be made manifest in the punishment of the wicked and the vindication of the righteous who have remained faithful.

Modified Apocalyptic Dualism

Why is there evil (and suffering) in the world? That question
raises a further question about the omnipotence or sovereignty
of God. Is there some area or sphere in which God's power is
absent or not complete? In expressing skepticism about the
validity of the law of retribution, Qoheleth never goes on to
explain why and how there is evil (and suffering) in the world.
In warning against trying to impose a human definition of justice on divine justice, the Book of Job raises few questions about
God's omnipotence. While the Book of Daniel presents God as
allowing the temporary triumph of arrogant foreign rulers, it
does not explore the underlying theological implications.

One early Jewish attempt at putting together the reality of
evil and suffering with the omnipotence of God can be
described as modified apocalyptic dualism. This approach proposes that while the world was created by God, it is now under
the direction of two subordinate powers (one good and the
other evil) until, at the time appointed by God, evil and the suffering associated with it will be destroyed forever. This
approach is a "dualism" insofar as it posits two opposing powers.
It is "modified" because it insists on the ultimate sovereignty of
God over all creation. And it is "apocalyptic" since it conveys a
revelation about the future course of history.

A first step toward modified apocalyptic dualism can be
discerned in Ben Sira's doctrine of the pairs: "Look at all the
works of the Most High: they come in pairs, one the opposite
of the other" (Sirach 33:15). Ben Sira reaches this conclusion by
first reflecting (somewhat artificially) on the calendar: "Why is
one day more important than another?" (33:7–9) Then he considers how some humans, although they share a common origin
("the ground . . . the dust"), are "blessed and exalted" whereas
others are "cursed and brought low" (33:10–13). Finally, Ben
Sira articulates his doctrine of the pairs: "Good is the opposite
of evil, and life is the opposite of death, so the sinner is the
opposite of the godly" (33:14). Ben Sira never doubts the good-

ness of God or of creation (see 39:16, 33). And yet he perceives a certain dualism in the very fabric of creation.

The clearest and most complete presentation of modified apocalyptic dualism appears in one of the Dead Sea scrolls, the Rule of the Community 3:13–4:23. Here the "instructor" explains the present and future course of history to the "sons of light," most likely junior members of a Jewish religious community of Essenes. His starting point is the absolute sovereignty of the God of Israel: "From the God of knowledge comes all that is and shall be. . . . The laws of all things are in his hand, and he provides them with all their needs." However, in creating humankind to govern the world, God has also appointed two spirits—the spirit of truth and the spirit of falsehood—in which humans are to walk until the time of his visitation, the definitive intervention of God.

In the present there is a clear division or dualism at all levels: "All the children of righteousness are ruled by the Prince of Light and walk in the ways of light, but all the children of falsehood are ruled by the Angel of Darkness and walk in the ways of darkness." The Angel of Darkness is a "Satan" figure (but more powerful and sinister than in the Book of Job), while the Angel of Light seems to be Michael or some similar figure.

The Angel of Darkness leads his people into all kinds of vices: greed, lying, deceit, lewd conduct, and so forth. Their visitation (or judgment) will involve "everlasting damnation by the avenging wrath of the fury of God, eternal torment, and endless disgrace together with shameful extinction in the fire of the dark regions." The Angel of Light will instill in his people all kinds of virtues: a spirit of humility, patience, abundant charity, unending goodness, understanding, and so forth. Their visitation (or judgment) will bring healing, great peace in a long life, fruitfulness, eternal joy, "a crown of glory, and a garment of majesty in unending light."

At the "visitation" God will once again show his countenance, take charge of all creation, and destroy falsehood along with the Angel of Darkness and the children of darkness forever.

Then truth "shall arise in the world forever," and God will shed the "spirit of truth" and the "spirit of purification." What is envisioned at the visitation is not the end of the world, but rather a restored world freed from evil and suffering, a new creation with no more tears or sadness.

This schema of modified apocalyptic dualism preserves the omnipotence of God by suggesting that even though the present is controlled by two subordinate powers, God exercises ultimate sovereignty from creation to the final visitation. It preserves the justice of God by deferring its definitive manifestation to the final visitation. It preserves the law of retribution by insisting that at the final visitation the righteous will be rewarded and the wicked will be punished. And so it explains the presence of evil and suffering in the world.

How do you know which group you are in? The instructor admits that everyone has some share in both groups, but goes on to say that it depends on "whether each one's portion in their two divisions is great or small." A later Jewish teaching sees in each person both a good inclination and an evil inclination, and contends that one's destiny depends on which inclination predominates.

Possibilities and Problems

Apocalyptic is the literature of dispossessed and suffering people. Indeed some scholars claim that only economically deprived and politically oppressed people can understand it. The basic theological affirmation of apocalyptic is that God is the only real source of security. Apocalyptic challenges us to trust in the fidelity of the God of love and mercy, rather than relying on money, power, or social status. Its theological perspective can help to place our sufferings in their proper perspective, to encourage people not to be overwhelmed by their sufferings, and to imagine the possibility of a better future. Apocalyptic is preeminently a theology of hope.

Although many images and ideas in Jewish apocalyptic seem strange to people today, this kind of literature has exercised an enormous impact on Jewish and Christian theology. Indeed Jewish apocalyptic has been aptly called "the mother of Christian theology." Jesus' proclamation of the coming kingdom of God as well as his eschatological discourses (Mark 13; Matthew 24–25; Luke 21) are steeped in apocalyptic. Paul's theology shares the framework of modified apocalyptic dualism with the Qumran Rule of the Community. It is, in fact, the key to understanding Paul's letter to the Romans. And the Book of Revelation is a full-scale Christian apocalypse.

Developed in the crucible of suffering, apocalyptic affirms the God of Israel as the Lord of all, takes sin seriously, makes room for evil and a "Satan" figure, and looks forward in hope to real freedom and the perfect service of God. It provides the context for important theological concepts such as resurrection and immortality, the last judgment, and eternal life with God in the kingdom of God. Apocalyptic is also the horizon against which Christians live their lives. The Lord's Prayer ("thy kingdom come") is an apocalyptic prayer. And all the New Testament writers emphasize constant vigilance and patient endurance as we await the fullness of God's kingdom and live out its present or inaugurated dimensions.

However, the apocalyptic solution is not without its own problems. Apart from the strange language and the peculiar ideas, there is the issue of unfulfilled prophecies. The author of the Book of Daniel expected that God, through the archangel Michael, would intervene soon and crush Antiochus Epiphanes and his supporters. In fact, it was the military activities of Judas Maccabeus that succeeded in restoring the traditional worship to the Jerusalem temple. Likewise, the Essene community at Qumran looked for a cosmic battle and an angelic army to rescue them. In fact, they were destroyed by the Roman army in A.D. 70.

Another objection to the apocalyptic solution is that in deferring salvation to the future it may encourage disinterest in the present. In fact, the apocalyptic texts (especially those in the New Testament) insist on constant vigilance and appropriate action in the present. Nevertheless, there is a tendency to live so much in the future or in heaven that one neglects the real problems of the present. This attitude can lead one to ignore or deny the reality of suffering, and even to fail to alleviate suffering where this is possible.

Finally, there is the difficulty of discernment. Some people see the present situation of "this world" as basically good, whereas others view it as corrupt and on the edge of destruction. For the former apocalyptic is crazy, whereas for the latter it is quite reasonable. Who is correct?

Questions for Reflection, Discussion, and Prayer

1. What elements of apocalyptic are part of your theology? What help do they provide you in understanding and coping with suffering?

2. How would the conflicts and contests in Daniel 1–6 have encouraged suffering Jews in the second century B.C.?

3. What assumptions about God and history underlie the visions in Daniel 7–12?

4. What does the lament in Daniel 8 contribute to understanding the causes of the people's sufferings?

5. What seems valid and what seems problematic in the schema of modified apocalyptic dualism?

Chapter Six

Jesus and the
Kingdom of God

"The kingdom of God is among you."
—Luke 17:21

ACCORDING TO the New Testament writers, the public ministry of Jesus was the presence (or at least the inauguration) of the kingdom of God among us on earth. What the writers of the Book of Daniel and the Dead Sea scrolls looked forward to in hope, the early Christians experienced as a present reality. Nevertheless, there were also continuities between Jewish apocalyptic and the ministry of the earthly Jesus. Indeed the context for that ministry was the apocalyptic concept of the kingdom of God, and much in Jesus' life and teachings is intelligible only through the lens of Jewish apocalyptic.

As we saw in the preceding chapter, Jewish apocalyptic had its origins in the suffering of God's people and was intended as a solution to or at least an explanation of suffering. This chapter first examines how Jesus understood the kingdom of God and his place within it. Then, against that background, we will look at two aspects of suffering: the suffering that Jesus' disciples can expect in the service of God's kingdom, and the physical and spiritual/psychological suffering that Jesus alleviated through his healing ministry.

In the first case, Jesus challenges his followers to accept what could be described as sufferings—loss of family and stable abode, traveling from place to place, dependence on others to maintain even a simple lifestyle, and opposition and persecution from outsiders—and to subordinate these sufferings to the greater task of sharing in Jesus' mission of proclaiming God's kingdom. In the second case, Jesus brings healing to persons suffering from various diseases and spiritual maladies as a sign of the presence of God's kingdom in his ministry.

The Kingdom of God

In the New Testament the "kingdom of God" refers to God's future display of power over all creation and the acknowledgment of it by all created things. The Lord's Prayer (Matthew 6:9–13; Luke 11:2–4) is preeminently a call for the full coming of God's reign—when God's will is to be done as perfectly on earth as it is in heaven.

The idea has its roots in the Old Testament concept of God's reign over all the earth (see Psalms 93, 96–97, 99), perhaps celebrated annually in ancient Israel to mark the beginning of the new year. In early Judaism the focus shifted from the present reign of God to the future display of God's reign. The shift was very likely associated with the continuing political subjugation of Israel after the return from exile in the sixth century B.C. God's ancient promises to Israel remain in effect but are put off to the future "day of the Lord." When the course of Israel's history has been accomplished (and that should be soon), God will intervene to vindicate the faithful within Israel by destroying evil and evildoers and by creating a new heaven and a new earth where God's will prevails. It is the task of God to bring about this kingdom and to make it visible to all. There are many different scenarios as to how this will come about, and not all of them involve a Messiah figure.

The parables of the kingdom of God in the Gospels have much in common with other Jewish writings of their time. They teach that the kingdom belongs to God, is in the future, and marks a decisive change from the present. Some sayings in the gospel tradition (Mark 9:1; 13:30; Matthew 10:23) suggest that Jesus and his early followers thought that the fullness of God's kingdom would come very soon. But other texts (Luke 11:20; 17:21; Matthew 11:12) indicate that the kingdom is enough of a present reality so that one can speak of it as "already" being here, as anticipated or inaugurated in and through Jesus' ministry.

A parable is a story taken from everyday life or ordinary experience. It uses figurative speech (similes or metaphors) to compare one thing to another. There is usually a strange or unusual feature, leading the hearer to suspect that this is no ordinary story and to try to discover what the story is really about.

The Gospels contain many parables, with large clusters in Mark 4, Matthew 13, 24–25, and Luke 8. Many of the parables are prefaced with the notice "the kingdom of God (or heaven) is like (or may be compared to)." The kingdom of God seems to have been the central theme of Jesus' preaching and to have provided the theological context for his ethical instructions (showing how to behave in light of the coming kingdom) and healings (as signs of the kingdom already here among us). In these narratives, many biblical scholars believe, one can hear the "voice" of Jesus.

Matthew 13:1–52 is a revised and expanded version of Mark 4:1–34. The early parts of Matthew 13 make clear various dimensions of the kingdom of God: the mixed reception of Jesus' proclamation of the kingdom (see 13:3–9, 18–23), the contrast between the kingdom's small beginnings in the present and its great conclusion (13:31–33), and the attitude of patient tolerance in expectation of its fullness and the accompanying final judgment (13:24–30, 36–43).

The discourse in Matthew 13 comes to a close with three short parables (13:44–50). These can provide an entry to Jesus' teaching about the kingdom and about the conduct appropriate to those who seek after it.

> 44 The kingdom of heaven is like treas-
> ure hidden in a field, which someone
> found and hid; then in his joy he goes
> and sells all that he has and buys that
> field.
> 45 Again, the kingdom of heaven is like
> a merchant in search of fine pearls; 46 on
> finding one pearl of great value, he went
> and sold all that he had and bought it.
> 47 Again, the kingdom of heaven is like
> a net that was thrown into the sea and
> caught fish of every kind; 48 when it was
> full, they drew it ashore, sat down, and
> put the good into baskets and threw out
> the bad. 49 So it will be at the end of the
> age. The angels will come out and sepa-
> rate the evil from the righteous 50 and
> throw them into the furnace of fire,
> where there will be weeping and gnash-
> ing of teeth.

The parables of the treasure buried in the field (Matthew 13:44) and the fine pearl (13:45–46) have the same basic structure. The one who comes upon them recognizes their surpassing value, makes a total commitment to obtaining them, and takes every means toward that goal. The parable of the net thrown into the sea consists of the story proper (13:47–48) and an explanation (13:49–50). Whether the interpretation circulated originally with the parable or was added later (which is more likely), it serves to underscore the theme of divine judgment as part of God's coming kingdom. The search for God's kingdom in the present transcends all the obstacles and sufferings that may stand in the way. And the fullness of God's kingdom will bring perfect happiness for the righteous and just punishment for the wicked.

All three parables fit the context of first-century Palestine, and would have been intelligible (though intriguing and a little puzzling) to persons taught by Jesus. People buried valuables in fields to avoid their being stolen; some merchants dealt in precious stones; and commercial fishermen (like Jesus' first disciples) regularly used dragnets. All three parables begin with the notice "the kingdom of heaven is like . . . ," thus warning us about their real topic—a topic that was very important at least in some Jewish theological and religious circles in Jesus' day.

The parables of the treasure and the pearl bring out the surpassing value of God's kingdom and the total commitment that it deserves and demands. The parable of the net (and its explanation) suggests that the full coming of God's kingdom will be accompanied by a universal judgment in which the righteous will be vindicated and rewarded and the wicked will be condemned and punished (or annihilated).

Throughout Christian history the kingdom of God has been identified in various ways. The saying in Luke 17:21 ("the kingdom of God is among you") has historically led many to an individual and spiritual interpretation ("the kingdom of God is within you") that is not true to the social and indeed cosmic dimensions of the kingdom according to Scripture. When Christianity, under the emperor Constantine, became the official religion of the Roman Empire, it was inevitable that God's kingdom would be identified with the dominant political structures. And this identification has been repeated many times over. But this approach ignores the transcendent aspect of kingdom; it is God's kingdom to bring, and what God will bring will surpass any earthly kingdom. It has also been tempting to identify the kingdom as the church. While the church bears witness to God's kingdom, tries to live out its values, and hopes and prays for its full coming, it is not really identical with the kingdom of God.

Each of these three interpretations of the kingdom—the individual-spiritual, the political, and the ecclesiastical—has some truth to it. Nevertheless, no one of them is entirely true to the eschatological kingdom proclaimed by Jesus and witnessed in the Gospels. If we want to be faithful to the biblical tradition, we need to recover the transcendent, future-present, and eschatological dimensions of the kingdom of God. If we want to make use of the biblical teachings about the kingdom of God, we need to recognize the kingdom of God as the horizon against which we live our Christian lives. It is not something we bring about; God brings it about. In the meantime we await it with hope for the fullness of that kingdom and try to act in a way that is appropriate to its claims. The kingdom is the horizon against which Christian life is to be lived, and it is the goal toward which all must point. It provides a theological context in which suffering can be understood.

The Gospels offer many motivations for doing "the right thing." Some texts appeal to the authority and example of Jesus (see Matthew 10:37–39), and others urge us to imitate the example of God who shows love for evildoers (see Matthew 5:43–48) and to fulfill God's will made manifest in the Scriptures and interpreted by Jesus (see Matthew 5:17–20). But modern readers tend to ignore the many appeals for right action based on the promise of rewards in the future and the present (see Mark 10:29–31). Many parables (see especially Matthew 24–25) urge a constant vigilance in the present against the horizon of the coming kingdom. The kingdom's coming is certain— but the precise time of its coming is known only to God (see Mark 13:32; Matthew 24:36). Therefore the proper response is to be prepared always, to act as if the kingdom with its final judgment were to come in the very next moment. If one wants to be ready for the last judgment and avoid the just punishment for sin that it involves, then one should live always in the shadow of God's kingdom. The believer's attitude, however, can and should be hopeful rather than fearful: "Now when these things begin to take place, stand erect and raise your heads, because your redemption is drawing near" (Luke 21:28). The last judgment will be a time of vindication rather than a time of condemnation for the righteous faithful.

It is not adequate to the biblical tradition to ignore the eschatological dimensions of God's kingdom or to explain them away as simply primitive religious imagery. Rather, in the context of New Testament theology, the kingdom of God is the place where God the creator and lord of all and Jesus as the proclaimer and sign of the kingdom of God join together.

Instructions for Disciples: Expect Suffering

In the gospel tradition, the first disciples called by Jesus have an exemplary significance, both positive and negative. The first four disciples are fishermen—Simon Peter and Andrew, James and John (see Mark 1:16–20; Matthew 4:18–22; Luke 5:1–11). As such they would have enjoyed a relatively stable existence in the present and decent prospects for the future, since commercial fishing in the Sea of Galilee was (and is) a fairly prosperous business enterprise. There is no indication that they had ever met Jesus or even knew anything about him. This serves to highlight the extraordinary power of Jesus' call and the attractiveness of his person. Moreover, the usual Jewish pattern by which students became associated with a master teacher was by their seeking out the teacher. However, by the power of his word alone ("follow me and I will make you fish for people," Mark 1:17), Jesus chooses and gathers to himself the disciples who will be with him throughout his public ministry. The disciples in turn leave behind their families, business, and stable lives to follow Jesus and share his mission. For the sake of the kingdom they were willing to suffer much. For them it was the "treasure" and the "pearl of great value."

The instruction to the Twelve about their mission according to Luke 9:1–6 (see Mark 6:7–13) appears toward the end of the Luke account of Jesus' ministry in Galilee (4:14–9:50). Based on various sources (Mark, the Sayings Source Q, and special Lukan material), this part of Luke's Gospel presents Jesus as a teacher, especially in the Sermon on the Plain in Luke 6:20–49 and in the parables discourse in Luke 8:1–18, as well as a powerful healer (see 5:12–26, 7:1–10) who is able even to restore the dead to life (7:11–17, 8:49–56) and to have control over a storm at sea (8:22–25), demons (8:26–39), and chronic illness (8:40–56).

Luke 9:1–6 describes the mission of the Twelve Apostles as the extension of Jesus' own mission of teaching and healing. A similar passage appears in Luke 10:1–12, in which a group of seventy (or seventy-two) disciples is appointed to prepare the way for Jesus as he and his followers make their way to Jerusalem in the journey narrative (9:51–19:44). The fact that the two instructions are so much alike suggests that they were intended for a larger circle than that constituted by the Twelve Apostles.

1 Then Jesus called the twelve together and gave them power and authority over all demons and to cure diseases, 2 and he sent them out to proclaim the kingdom of God and to heal.

3 He said to them, "Take nothing for your journey, no staff, nor bag, nor bread, nor money—not even an extra tunic. 4 Whatever house you enter, stay there, and leave from there. 5 Wherever they do not welcome you, as you are leaving that town shake the dust off from your feet as a testimony against them."

⁶ They departed and went through the villages, bringing the good news and curing diseases everywhere.

The "mission of the Twelve" consists of a narrative framework (9:1–2, 6) and an instruction (9:3–5). In the first part of the narrative (9:1–2) Jesus determines to share his powers as a teacher and healer, and in the concluding section (9:6) the Twelve set out on their mission. In Luke's two-volume narrative, the Twelve Apostles serve as an important principle of continuity between the ministry of the earthly Jesus and the early days of the church in Jerusalem after Jesus' resurrection and ascension (see Acts 1–9). Here they are called to do what Jesus does in his ministry and to share actively in his mission from God.

The instruction (9:3–5) assumes that the Twelve Apostles will be on the move as they carry forward Jesus' mission. According to 9:3, they are to avoid all unnecessary baggage ("no staff, nor bag, nor bread, nor money . . . ") and to place their trust totally in God to provide for their needs. On the practical level (9:4), they are to rely on the hospitality and generosity of those whom they encounter and who accept them into their households. Rather than spending time and energy on seeking better accommodations, the Twelve Apostles are told to be satisfied with what is first given them by their hosts. If and when they meet opposition and rejection (9:5), their proper response is for them to move on peacefully, with only a symbolic and nonviolent gesture of leave-taking: "Shake the dust off your feet as a testimony against them."

These instructions fit the context of first-century Palestine and of the Greco-Roman world in general. Their philosophies and religions were spread by traveling missionaries who either begged for food and support or relied more subtly on help and hospitality from others along the way. What is distinctive about Luke 9:1–6 and other such texts in the Gospels is the specific religious context in which the instructions are set. The truly important tasks are proclaiming the kingdom of God and healing as a sign of its presence. Their simple lifestyle is entirely in the service of the mission, subordinate to and useful only as a help toward preaching God's kingdom in word and deed. It is not undertaken merely as a kind of asceticism.

The essence of Christian discipleship is to be with Jesus and to share his mission (see Mark 3:14). The simple lifestyle recommended in the various missionary discourses (Mark 6:7–13; Matthew 10:1–42; Luke 9:1–6; 10:1–12) is in the service of sharing in Jesus' proclamation of God's kingdom and healing those in need.

The absolute and radical claims involved in following Jesus may demand separation from one's natural family and becoming part of the "new family" of Jesus (see Mark 3:31–35). At the very beginning of Luke's journey narrative, Jesus refuses the requests of prospective disciples to bury a father or to say farewell to those at home (see 9:59–62). In a culture in which family ties and obligations were enormously important, this was powerful teaching. Indeed Jesus promises division within the household (see Luke 12:51–53) and even urges prospective disciples to "hate" their family members (see Luke 14:26).

These family tensions are illustrated by the case of Jesus himself. According to Mark 3:21, members of his own family try to restrain him on the grounds that people were saying "He has gone out of his mind," thus bringing shame upon the entire family. In response, Jesus redefines his family as "whoever does the will of God" (Mark 3:35). His disciples—those dedicated to his ideals and mission—now constitute the family of Jesus.

The disciples, especially the Twelve Apostles but also presumably the wider circle, are promised rewards not only in the present but also "in the age to come" (Mark 10:28–31). But the same text also promises them "sufferings." During Jesus' public ministry they have the benefit of receiving Jesus' wisdom and even his foreknowledge of the suffering that awaits him and them. Nevertheless, in all the Gospels they are more or less obtuse and, instead of growing in spiritual insight, they regress on the way from Galilee to Jerusalem. They have a particular difficulty in understanding and accepting Jesus' predictions of his own suffering and death (see Mark 8:31, 9:31, 10:33–34). In Jerusalem, when Jesus is arrested, they scatter, and Peter denies Jesus three times. By contrast, the women followers emerge as the faithful ones when they witness Jesus' death and burial, and go to his tomb on Easter Sunday.

The major problem posed by these gospel texts is their applicability or transfer to Christians beyond the first century. Or, to the put the same point in another way, can we use Jesus' instructions to his disciples in Christian life today?

In the Christian tradition there has been a long-standing debate on this issue. Some contend that the discipleship teachings are incumbent on all Christians. Others make a distinction between a Christian elite and ordinary Christians. From the perspective of biblical studies today, the question is often posed and treated in a historical framework. Some would argue that the extreme teachings about discipleship—especially the simple lifestyle and the separation from family—pertain only to the mission of the historical Jesus in first-century rural Palestine. Others argue that the teachings about lack of family, possessions, and stable abode best fit the rural conditions of the earliest days of the post-Easter Christian mission. In both periods those who proclaimed the kingdom of God went from place to place, dependent upon the hospitality and generosity of the local population.

The link between the very concrete instructions most at home in first-century Palestine and the generalizing tendency in the Christian theological tradition is best found in the editorial work of the Evangelists. Each gospel writer used traditional materials in a new urban context outside the land of Israel: Mark in Rome around A.D. 70, Matthew in Antioch around A.D. 85–90, Luke perhaps in Greece around A.D. 85–90, and John in Syria or Ephesus or Transjordan around A.D. 90. They all faced the challenge of translation or transfer, and each of them gave distinctive emphases to the discipleship tradition: success and failure along the way (Mark), learning from Jesus the teacher

(Matthew), carrying on the message and work of Jesus (Luke), and bearing witness to Jesus as the revealer and the revelation of God (John).

The very process of interpretation and development as illustrated by the Evangelists provides the bridge between discipleship in Jesus' time and in other times and places. It is neither possible nor useful to imitate Jesus' lifestyle in all its details, or to try to put into practice all the concrete instructions that he gave to his first followers. But one can and should discern some core values in the discipleship passages in the Gospels—absolute dedication to God's kingdom, a sharing in Jesus' mission, a simple lifestyle, a willingness to subordinate or forgo human ties and physical comforts, and the assurance of opposition and suffering for the sake of the gospel—that can give shape to Christian discipleship in any age and place. These core values can serve as the starting points for reflecting on the place of Jesus' teachings on discipleship in Christian life today.

Healing as a Sign of God's Kingdom: Suffering Alleviated

Besides the teachings of Jesus and the passion narratives, the Gospels present many accounts of extraordinary displays of power by Jesus. These "miracles" fall into several different categories: healings, exorcisms, nature miracles, and restorations of dead persons to life.

Especially prominent in the Gospels are stories in which Jesus heals persons suffering from various forms of physical illnesses or from chronic conditions: paralysis (Mark 2:1–12; 3:1–6; Luke 13:10–17; John 5:1–9), blindness (Mark 8:22–26; 10:46–52; John 9:1–41), leprosy (Mark 1:40–45; Luke 17:11–17), and other conditions (Mark 1:29–31; 5:24–34; 7:31–37; Luke 14:1–6; 22:49–51). There are also many cases in which Jesus heals persons suffering from a spiritual or psychological malady that the Gospels describe as possession by a demon (Mark 1:23–28, 5:1–20, 7:24–30, 9:14–29; Matthew 9:32–33; Luke 8:2). In these cases Jesus brings physical or spiritual healing to persons who were undergoing serious suffering.

The very short account of Jesus healing Peter's mother-in-law, in Mark 1:29–31, illustrates the basic dynamics of the healing stories in the Gospels.

> 29 As soon as they left the synagogue, they entered the house of Simon and Andrew, with James and John. 30 Now Simon's mother-in-law was in bed with a fever, and they told him about her at once. 31 He came and took her by the hand and lifted her up. Then the fever left her, and she began to serve them.

Part of Mark's account about the early days of Jesus' public ministry in Galilee, this story is set in Capernaum, at the house of Simon and Andrew, the first two disciples called by Jesus (see Mark 1:16–18). We are given a brief description of the woman's condition: "Simon's mother-in-law was in bed with a fever" (Mark 1:30). The fact that the four disciples inform Jesus about her condition suggests that they believed that he might be able to do something about it. In almost every Gospel healing story there is some display of faith, either by the sick persons themselves or by their friends. Jesus heals the woman by his own power: "He came and took her by the hand and lifted her up." He does not merely intercede for her in prayer. Her healing is immediate and complete: "the fever left her." The healing is proven by the woman's ability to return immediately to her normal tasks. Everything in this short narrative highlights the superhuman power of Jesus as a healer.

Jesus is not the only healer in the Bible. The Israelite prophets Elijah and Elisha in 1 Kings 17–2 Kings 13 perform many miracles, including some healings. But they usually pray to God for help, and the miracles take place through their intercession. Likewise, Hanina ben Dosa, a Galilean Jewish teacher contemporary with Jesus, also developed a reputation as a miracle worker. But he, too, acts more as a powerful intermediary with God rather than as the source of his own power. In the Acts of the Apostles, the miracles carried out by the apostles follow the pattern set by Jesus in Luke's Gospel and are understood as manifestations of his power. What is striking in the Gospel miracle stories is that Jesus acts on his own authority and not simply as an intermediary of God's power. Since Jesus does what God does, the miracle stories hint at the divinity of Jesus.

The healing stories in the Gospels contain some elements of theological interpretation. For example, in Mark 1:29–31 the statements that Jesus "lifted her up" and that Peter's mother-in-law began to "serve" them use Greek terms that very likely evoked the themes of resurrection and ministry, respectively, in the minds of Mark's first readers. Nevertheless, a good case can be made for the basic historicity of many of the miracle stories in the Gospels. The miracles are prominent in all the Gospels and their sources. They fit well with Jesus' proclamation of God's kingdom. And yet, because Jesus acts on his own authority and displays his own power, they differ from the miracle stories told about Elijah and Elisha and about Hanina ben Dosa. Moreover, these miracles exposed Jesus to the charge that he was acting out of the devil's power rather than out of God's power.

This last consideration indicates the need for interpreting Jesus' miracles and for situating them in the context of Jesus' proclamation of the kingdom of God. The Gospels contain many stories about Jesus' healings, exorcisms, nature miracles, and restorations to life. And yet to describe Jesus as merely or primarily a miracle worker would give a false impression of the Gospels and of Jesus. Rather, the miracles must be viewed in the context of his proclamation of God's kingdom. They are signs that in Jesus' ministry the kingdom of God was already present or at least inaugurated.

In Jesus' own time the meaning of his miracles was controversial. While his opponents did not deny his power to heal and work other miracles, they did dispute the origin of his power. According to Luke 11:15–23, the opponents charged that Jesus "casts out demons by Beelzebul, the prince of demons." The thrust of Jesus' response was to show how absurd it would be to suppose that Jesus could perform exorcisms if he really were an agent of Satan. On the contrary, Jesus affirms that he is on the side of God and that his miracles indicate the presence of God's reign: "But if it is by the finger of God that I cast out the demons, then the kingdom of God has come to you" (Luke 11:20).

Jesus was the prophet of God's kingdom, not a magician or a faith-healer or a medical doctor. His healings and other miracles point to the presence of God's reign and to his role as its prophet. His mighty acts are part of his mission to God's people. They are a summons to faith, and so faith is an element in almost all the Gospel miracle stories.

Through his healing activities Jesus alleviated the sufferings of God's people. Why then did Jesus not heal everyone in need? That question misses the point of Jesus' miracles and his role as the prophet of God's kingdom. His healings were signs pointing toward the fullness of God's kingdom, where there will be no more suffering. But for now, suffering remains part of human existence.

Possibilities and Problems

These reflections on the mission of Jesus' disciples and on Jesus' healings and exorcisms highlight the overriding significance of the kingdom of God not only in Jesus' ministry but also in Christian life.

In his missionary discourses, Jesus challenges his disciples to take hardship and suffering upon themselves as they participate in Jesus' mission of preaching and healing. Rather than being overwhelmed by the difficulties, his disciples are urged to transcend them in the name of dedication to what Jesus regarded as the most important entity of all—the kingdom of God. By subordinating their sufferings to a higher ideal, they (and we) can place present sufferings in their proper perspective. It is amazing what Christians have done through the centuries in overcoming hardships and sufferings out of their dedication to the ideals of Jesus and in their response to his call.

In his healings of sick and possessed persons, Jesus manifests the power of God's kingdom already at work among us. And there is no reason to conclude that Jesus' healing power was confined only to the time of Jesus or to the apostolic age. There is a long history of miraculous healings that apparently transcend explanation solely in terms of human causality. Their manifestations range from healing centers like Lourdes to evangelical meetings that proclaim, "Expect a miracle." And the testimonies to these healings, in turn, continue to inspire suffering people with hope for healing.

And yet on both fronts there are problems. The first followers of Jesus were not entirely successful in facing up to the challenges of discipleship. If we follow Mark's narrative, the disciples start out well: They respond immediately and generously to Jesus' call; they accompany him in his ministry; and they are sent out by him to extend his ministry. But as he moves toward Jerusalem, their failure to understand the mystery of the cross and to accept Jesus' identity as the suffering Messiah becomes acute. Faced with the mystery of his passion and death, they flee. Only the women disciples remain faithful during the passion. The point is that subordinating one's hardships and sufferings to the kingdom of God is not easy. The negative example of Jesus' first followers provides a lesson in humility for all prospective disciples of Jesus. The challenge "Are you able to drink the cup that I drink?" (Mark 10:38) remains a warning against presuming too readily on one's own ability to endure suffering in the service of God's kingdom.

The slogan, "Expect a miracle," while a source of hope to some, is discouraging to others. What happens when the miracle does not come? Persons with physical disabilities or chronic psychiatric conditions are teaching the church today about some of the problems that they have endured from "miracles" theology. Many have been taken to faith healers without positive result. The negative result is often a sense of guilt: "Perhaps I didn't pray hard enough" or "Maybe I don't have enough faith." And most important of all is the idea that there is something "wrong" with disabled persons. It may be sounder theology to regard the disability as an integral part of this person's identity as a child of God. In the final analysis we have to leave miraculous healing (or nonhealing) where it belongs—in the hands of God. But we also need to be sensitive to the theological insights of disabled persons about "miracles" theology.

Questions for Reflection, Discussion, and Prayer

1. What is different about Jesus' understanding of the kingdom of God compared to the apocalyptic approaches taken in the Book of Daniel and the Dead Sea scrolls?

2. What sufferings are Jesus' disciples expected to endure as they share in his mission of proclaiming God's kingdom?

3. What do the failures of Jesus' first followers in accepting the mystery of the cross tell you about discipleship?

4. What is the theological significance of Jesus' healings and exorcisms? In what sense are they signs of God's kingdom?

5. Do you understand the problems that a disabled person might have with "miracles" theology?

Chapter Seven

Death and Resurrection

"Was it not necessary that the Messiah should suffer these things and then enter into his glory?"

—Luke 24:26

FOR MANY CHRISTIANS the cross or the crucifix symbolizes Jesus' passion and the entire paschal mystery. When my mother lay dying and could no longer speak, the crucifix in her hospital room became the focus of my thoughts and prayers. That symbol helped me place her suffering and death in the context of her life of Christian faith and in the context of Jesus' life, death, and resurrection. Never had the crucifix been so meaningful to me.

The word *passion* is part of the Christian vocabulary. We speak of the "passion" of Jesus and of Passion Week. However, we may forget that the word "passion" means "suffering," derived from the Greek and Latin terms for suffering. The passion of Jesus concerns his suffering and death, and our participation in it.

Another part of the Christian vocabulary is the *paschal mystery*. This derives from the Hebrew word for "Passover." Applied to Jesus, it refers to his suffering, death, and resurrection. It evokes the symbolism of the Passover Lamb and the theological themes of the perfect sacrifice leading to redemption from the slavery of sin and death. One of the earliest confessions of Christian faith (1 Corinthians 15:3–5) summarizes the paschal mystery in this way: "that Christ died for our sins in accordance with the scriptures, and that he was buried, and that he was raised on the third day in accordance with the scriptures, and that he appeared to Cephas, then to the twelve." The paschal mystery—Jesus' suffering, death, and resurrection—is the core of Christian faith. And at the core of the paschal mystery is the theme of suffering.

The early Christians who proclaimed Jesus as Messiah, Lord, and Son of God had to confront the facts that their hero was arrested, tried, and executed under the Roman governor, Pontius Pilate, in Jerusalem in the year A.D. 30. As the confession in 1 Corinthians 15:3–5 indicates, they interpreted Jesus' sufferings as fulfilling the Old Testament Scriptures and as a sacrifice for sins. But the basis for these interpretations was the fact of Jesus' death on Good Friday and the conviction that Jesus had been raised from the dead on Easter Sunday.

Hearing the words "death and resurrection," Christians instinctively think of the case of Jesus—and rightly so since, according to an early Christian hymn, Jesus is "the firstborn from the dead" (Colossians 1:18). However, the motif of the death and resurrection has a rich biblical background, especially in the later books of the Old Testament. And at the heart of that background is the mystery of suffering.

While the Book of Sirach presents a traditional and somewhat fatalistic approach to suffering and death, 2 Maccabees and Wisdom hold out the hope of overcoming innocent suffering through life after death. While 2 Maccabees stresses the physical dimension of this afterlife existence (the resurrection of the body), Wisdom emphasizes its spiritual dimension (the

souls of the righteous). Both books agree that the present sufferings of righteous persons will be transcended and overcome
by the power and justice of God made manifest in God's judgment upon the righteous and the wicked. To understand the
early Christian claims about Jesus' death and resurrection, we
need to look first at these Jewish texts.

Death and Resurrection in Judaism

In the Old Testament texts that we have studied so far there has
been little attention to life after death. Psalm 88 ("the gloomiest psalm") spoke about Sheol and "the Pit" as a place of darkness and oblivion where no one can praise God. At several
points Job raised the hope for life after death only to reject it as
worse than annihilation: "I loathe my life; I would not live forever" (7:16). The great exception was the Book of Daniel,
whose vision of history climaxes in the resurrection of the dead:
"Many of those who sleep in the dust of the earth shall awake,
some to everlasting life, and some to shame and everlasting contempt" (12:2).

During the second and first centuries B.C. there was an
increasing interest among Jews in life after death, and the result
was a variety of approaches. Whereas the Book of Daniel treats
resurrection as a collective and end-time event, other works
from roughly the same time, such as 2 Maccabees and the Wisdom of Solomon, deal with life after death on a more personal
and immediate level. In relation to the mystery of suffering,
however, the dynamic is the same. The idea is that after death
the righteous will be vindicated and the wicked will be punished, and so God's omnipotence and justice are preserved
because their manifestation is deferred.

By way of contrast it may be useful first to look at some
Jewish texts that convey a more traditional and skeptical
approach to life after death. In his instruction about mourning for
the dead, Ben Sira urges that grief be intense but circumscribed

("for one day, or two," Sirach 38:17). He is more concerned with the harmful effects of excessive grieving on the part of the living than he is about the fate of the dead. In fact, he warns mourners to recognize that "there is no coming back" (38:21) and to "remember his fate, for yours is like it; yesterday it was his, and today it is yours" (38:22). While Ben Sira does not deny outright the possibility of a meaningful afterlife, the most he can affirm is that the dead are "at rest" (38:23).

In another meditation on death (41:1–13), Ben Sira first considers how bitter death is to the prosperous and how welcome death is to the needy (41:1–2). He also notes that death is "the Lord's decree for all flesh" (41:4). Since death is inevitable, one must accept it. Whatever life after death may be, it has little significance: "there are no questions asked in Hades" (41:4).

Many people seek a kind of immortality through their children. But Ben Sira, in 41:5–10, reminds his readers that "those who have forsaken the law of the Most High God" (41:8) will surely produce wicked and shameful children. Through these "abominable children," sinners suffer perpetual disgrace, and their sinful offspring (children) bear the shame of their wicked parents and replicate their evil behavior.

In 41:11–13 Ben Sira expresses his positive ideal of immortality through a good and virtuous name: "a good name lasts forever" (41:13). A reputation for virtue lasts longer than the human body or the span of a human life or even gold: "a virtuous name will never be blotted out" (41:11).

Concerning life after death, Ben Sira remains cautious and even skeptical. Existence in Sheol is little better than annihilation. The attempt to attain immortality through one's offspring is doomed to failure unless one lives a virtuous life according to the Torah. The surest way to immortality is through earning a "good name" that lives on in the community's collective memory. Ben Sira's catalogue of biblical heroes ("now let us praise famous men") in chapters 44–50 illustrates his concept of immortality by memory.

Second Maccabees tells the story of the events leading up to the Maccabean revolt in 164 B.C. and the restoration of the traditional forms of worship in the Jerusalem temple. The Greek version included in the Catholic and Orthodox canons of the Bible is a digest of a five-volume work by Jason of Cyrene. The book as we have it was composed in the late second or early first century B.C. It concerns three attacks on the Jerusalem temple (3:1-40, 4:1–10:9, 10:10–15:36) and describes how God defended his temple and his people by miraculous means in the first instance and by Judas Maccabeus in the other two cases. The chief contributions of 2 Maccabees to the biblical understanding of suffering concern the martyr's death and belief in the resurrection of the dead.

A *martyr* is one who bears witness. It was originally a legal term for one who gave testimony at a trial. It became a religious word for those who willingly die for their religious convictions in part because of 2 Maccabees. The narrative setting is the same as that of the Book of Daniel—the persecution of Jews under Antiochus IV Epiphanes. This work contains short accounts about two women who were killed for having their sons circumcised and about a group of Jews who were burned in a cave for trying to observe the Sabbath (2 Maccabees 6:10–11). The author explains these sufferings as both a divine discipline and a divine punishment for Israel's sins (6:12–16).

The longer accounts about martyrdom involve the refusal by faithful Jews to eat pork. The elderly Eleazar, in 6:18–31, prefers "to die a good death willingly and nobly for the revered and holy laws" (6:28). The seven brothers and their mother (7:1–42) are brought forward to undergo terrible tortures and, at each point, they explain why they remain unwilling to eat "unlawful swine's flesh." In 14:37–46 Razis dies a gruesome death for "Judaism," because he prefers "to die nobly rather than to fall into the hands of sinners" (14:42). All these martyrs exhibit fidelity and courage in the face of death. In subordinating their suffering to their religious convictions, they help to define martyrdom and set a pattern for Jews and Christians alike.

According to 2 Maccabees, one reason for the martyrs' courage was their belief in the resurrection of the dead. The dialogues of the wicked king with the seven brothers and their mother in 2 Maccabees 7 revolve around the themes of resurrection and of rewards and punishments after death. The second brother asserts that "the King of the universe will raise us up to an everlasting renewal of life, because we have died for his laws" (7:9). The third brother offers his tongue and hands to the torturers because "I hope to get them back again" (7:11). The fourth brother threatens the king with the warning that for him "there will be no resurrection to life" (7:14). The martyrs offer themselves to the torturers because they believe that their caring and compassionate God will restore them to eternal life. They undergo these sufferings "because of our sins against our own God" (7:18), and yet they approach death with the full confidence that God will reward them with eternal life and will punish their persecutors by depriving them of "resurrection to life."

The author's convictions about resurrection led him to give a very interesting and influential interpretation to Judas Maccabeus's sin offering on behalf of Jewish soldiers who died in battle while wearing the tokens of pagan deities (2 Maccabees 12:39–45). Rather than taking Judas's offering as a means of purifying his army from the contamination of idolatry, the author presents it as a sacrifice made for the benefit of the dead: "He made atonement for the dead, so that they might be delivered from their sin" (12:46). He understands Judas's action as part of his belief in resurrection and suggests that the living can do something vicariously by way of expiation on behalf of the dead so that they too might have a share in "resurrection to life."

The Book of Wisdom was composed in Greek at Alexandria in Egypt in the first century B.C. It is more a book about wisdom—its benefits, nature, and role in history—than a Wisdom Book like Proverbs or Sirach. Its three main parts concern righteousness and immortality (chaps. 1–5), wisdom (chaps. 6–9), and wisdom's role in the early history of Israel (chaps. 10–19). The first part is especially pertinent to the theme of suffering.

The opening exhortation (1:1–15) begins with a call to "love righteousness" and ends with the assertion that "righteousness is immortal." It also contains a warning not to invite death by unrighteous behavior, especially idolatry.

The reflection on the errors of the wicked (1:16–2:24) accuses the "ungodly" of making a covenant with death and of living only according to their desires and pleasures because they suppose "there is no return from our death" (2:5). Since the righteous understand themselves as children of God, believe in immortality for the righteous, and act justly, they are a rebuke to the ungodly (2:12–17). The ungodly imagine that death will be the downfall of the righteous and so plot to subject righteous persons to trial and execution. They fail to grasp that eternal life with God is the "wages of holiness" and the "prize for blameless souls" (2:22).

The contrast between the destinies of the righteous and the wicked (3:1–12) revolves around the relation between righteousness and immortality. Whereas the wicked suppose that death is the end of human existence, in fact, "the souls of the righteous are in the hand of God" (3:1) and their hope is "full of immortality" (3:4). Whatever suffering the righteous endure is a discipline and a test from God (3:5–6). Their life after death (3:7–9), however, will be glorious: "they shine forth . . . like sparks" (see Daniel 12:1–3). They share in God's kingdom and live in God's truth, love, and mercy. The destiny of the wicked (3:10–12) is based on the principle that evildoing carries its own punishments: "their hope is vain, their labors are unprofitable" (3:11).

The reflection on childlessness (3:13–4:15) is a rebuttal of the attempt to obtain immortality through having children. It contends that "childlessness with virtue" (4:1) is preferable to the "prolific brood of the ungodly" (4:3). True immortality is not based on begetting many children but on a virtuous life, which is known to God and other discerning persons.

The contrast between the righteous and the ungodly (4:16–5:14) revolves around death and judgment. The righteous dead will judge the ungodly, and at the last judgment the wicked will recognize their sins and "the unexpected salvation of the righteous" (5:2). Then the wicked will admit that "we had no sign of virtue to show, but were consumed in our wickedness" (5:13).

The closing (5:15–23) stresses that immortality is a gift from God rather than a natural endowment due to the immortal soul. The righteous are immortal because God shows special care for them.

Whereas 2 Maccabees emphasizes the resurrection of the body, Wisdom deals more with the continuing existence of the soul ("the souls of the righteous are in the hand of God," 3:1). Two passages in the Book of Wisdom—about preexistent souls (8:19–20) and about the perishable body weighing down the soul (9:15)—indicate the possible influence of Greek philosophy on the author. This influence can be discerned also in passages that concern wisdom as the "world soul" (1:7), the cardinal virtues (8:7), divine providence (14:1–4), and the "scientific" basis for miracles (19:18–21). Nevertheless, the author's real interest in chapters 1–5 is more with the Jewish tradition and with the ethical and religious dimensions of suffering and happiness, righteous and unrighteous conduct, and rewards and punishments after death. His own approach is a variation on the apocalyptic solution. His description of the plot of the wicked against the suffering righteous one in 2:12–20 foreshadows what happens to Jesus not only in the passion narratives but also in the Gospels taken as a whole.

Jesus' Suffering and Death

It is often said that Mark's Gospel is a passion narrative with a long introduction. One can also say that everything in Mark's Gospel leads up to Jesus' passion and death. Jesus' death on the cross is the consequence of his being misunderstood and rejected by almost everyone. His sufferings are both physical and spiritual/psychological.

After telling us that Jesus is the Son of God (1:1–15), Mark describes Jesus' successes as a healer and a teacher (1:16–45) and shows how he outwitted his opponents in various controversies (2:1–3:6). But this first phase of Jesus' Galilean ministry ends with Jesus as the object of a plot against his life by the Pharisees and Herodians (3:6). The second phase of Jesus' Galilean ministry (3:7–6:6) begins with misunderstanding and opposition from the Jerusalem scribes and members of Jesus' family (3:20–35) and ends in the same way in his hometown (6:1–6). In the third phase (6:7–8:21) his disciples repeatedly fail to understand him, and their incomprehension is exposed by Jesus' questions in 8:14–21: "Do you still not perceive or understand?"

On the journey from Galilee to Jerusalem (8:22–10:52), Jesus foretells his suffering, death, and resurrection three times (8:31, 9:31, 10:33–34), only to be met at each point by the disciples' failure to grasp that he is the suffering Messiah. During his Jerusalem ministry (11:1–13:37) Jesus engages in debates with various opponents and, in his final discourse (chap. 13), he warns his followers about persecutions to come (13:9–13) and tells them to be on guard always (13:32–37). Almost everyone misunderstands and rejects Jesus, and his passion and death are the culmination of this process. Jesus, however, remains faithful to his mission of proclaiming God's kingdom in word and deed.

In the Markan passion narrative proper (chaps. 14–15) Jesus recognizes the suffering that awaits him and struggles to accept it (14:33–36). He is betrayed by Judas and abandoned by the rest of the Twelve. He is arrested, tried, and executed under Pontius Pilate, with the collaboration of the Jerusalem leaders. The crowds, who once showed positive enthusiasm for him (11:1–11), now reject him in favor of Barabbas (15:6–15). He dies a cruel death by crucifixion, with the psalm of the righteous sufferer (Psalm 22; Mark 15:34) on his lips. Only a few women followers remain at the foot of the cross (15:40–41).

That Jesus suffered not only in his final days but also throughout his public ministry is clear from Mark's Gospel, which is aptly called "the Gospel of Suffering." But why did Jesus suffer? Mark gives three basic answers. Perhaps in response to a persecution against his own community at Rome, Mark presents Jesus as a model of fidelity in the midst of suffering. Jesus shows compassion toward those who suffer (1:41, 3:5, 10:14), invites his disciples to take up the cross and so find real freedom (8:34–35), and gives a good example during his own final sufferings (14–15). Mark also suggests that Jesus' suffering and death constituted a vicarious and expiatory sacrifice: "to give his life as a ransom for many" (10:45); and "my blood of the covenant, which is poured out for many" (14:24). Moreover, Mark indicates that Jesus' suffering was part of God's plan, and that there is an element of divine necessity about his suffering and death: "the Son of Man must undergo great suffering" (8:31).

Matthew and Luke followed Mark's outline and his basic approach to Jesus' suffering and death. They also developed some dimensions of Jesus' suffering. By prefacing his Gospel with an infancy narrative (chaps. 1–2), Matthew showed that Jesus suffered opposition from the very beginning of his life, as the episodes in 2:1–23 indicate. Also, by including many Old Testament fulfillment quotations in his infancy narrative, Matthew prepared for his own increased emphasis on how Jesus fulfilled the Scriptures (and so also God's will) during his passion and death.

Luke, likewise, introduced the note of suffering into Jesus' infancy: "a sign that will be opposed" (2:34). And during his suffering on the cross, Jesus proves to be the perfect example of fidelity to his own principles. The one who challenged his followers to love their enemies prays to his Father to forgive those responsible for his death (23:34). The one who showed compassion for outcasts promises "the good thief" that "today you will be with me in Paradise" (23:43). And the one who urged total trust in God prays with the words of Psalm 31:5: "Father, into your hands I commend my spirit" (23:46).

John's Gospel follows a different outline and presents another perspective on Jesus' suffering and death. For John,

Jesus is the revealer of God and the revelation of God ("the Word"). In both the Book of Signs (chaps. 1–12) and the Book of Glory (chaps. 13–21), a major Johannine theme is that the "lifting up" of Jesus on the cross is really part of his exaltation to his heavenly Father: "When you have lifted up the Son of Man, then you will realize that I am he" (8:28). John places special emphasis on the paradox of Jesus' suffering and death. What seems to outsiders to be a terrible and total defeat is in fact a glorious victory. In the eyes of Pontius Pilate, Jesus is just another Jewish rebel pretending to be the Messiah. But to people of faith, Jesus really is "the King of the Jews" (see 18:28–19:16). John's stress on Jesus' suffering and death as a triumph comes from his viewing Jesus' suffering and death in the light of his resurrection.

The Resurrection of Jesus

An essential element in early Christian proclamations of faith was the affirmation that Jesus was raised from the dead and that he appeared to many of his disciples. These confessions are often stated in the passive voice ("he was raised"), with the implication that God had raised Jesus from the dead (the "theological passive"). The early Christians believed that the person who died on the cross was divinely restored to life. The life after death that Jesus experienced was not simply the immortality of his soul or even of his good name. Nor was it reanimation or resuscitation. Nor was it expected that Jesus, once having been restored to life, would die again as we presume was so in the cases of Lazarus, the son of the widow of Nain, and the daughter of Jairus. The early Christians believed that Jesus had really died and was restored by God to eternal life.

In his controversy with the Sadducees in Jerusalem (see Mark 12:18–27), Jesus sides with the Pharisees against the Sadducees by arguing for the resurrection of the dead. He contends that this belief can be found in the Torah ("I am the God of

Abraham, the God of Isaac, and the God of Jacob," see Exodus 3:6) and that resurrected life with God differs from earthly life ("like angels in heaven"). But with regard to other Jewish scenarios of the end-time, the resurrection of Jesus at Easter Sunday is unique. That an individual (and not all the dead or at least all the righteous) should be raised from the dead was not a usual apocalyptic expectation. According to Daniel 12:1–3, the resurrection is a collective or communal event at the end of history. But the Christian claim is that Jesus was raised from the dead at Easter, before the cosmic signs, the general resurrection, and the final judgment had taken place. Or, to put it more accurately, the resurrection of Jesus marks the beginning of a series of end-time or eschatological events. His resurrection is the most decisive moment yet in the present or inaugurated kingdom of God.

There is no direct description of Jesus' resurrection in the New Testament. Instead, what we have are stories about the empty tomb and the appearances of the risen Jesus. The empty tomb stories (Mark 16:1–8; Matthew 28:1–10; Luke 24:1–12; John 20:1–10), while they do not "prove" the resurrection, are at least the necessary presupposition for the early Christian claim that God raised Jesus from the dead. The appearance accounts (1 Corinthians 15:3–11; Matthew 28:11–20; Luke 24:13–49; John 20:11–21:23; Mark 16:9–20) provide the testimony of Jesus' disciples and friends that they encountered him as really alive again. Some of the appearance narratives emphasize the physical character of Jesus' risen body (he shares meals), while other accounts stress the spiritual dimensions (he suddenly appears in a locked house, as in John 20:19).

Another important witness to Jesus' resurrection was the transformation that his disciples underwent between the arrest of Jesus, when they all fled, and their fearless proclamation of Jesus' death and resurrection as the most important event in human history. If Jesus had not been raised from the dead, the proclamation of him as a wise teacher and a miracle worker would perhaps have been sufficient to insure the continuation of the Jesus movement. But Jesus' followers put forward the proclamation of Jesus' death and resurrection as the basis of all their beliefs about Jesus and God. The empty tomb, the appearances, and the spread of the gospel provide the best evidence for faith in Jesus' resurrection.

The resurrection represents the vindication of Jesus as the righteous sufferer and servant of God, and gives hope to all who believe in him. Although Jesus' suffering and death appeared to be a tragic defeat ("My God, my God, why have you forsaken me?" Psalm 22:1), the resurrection transformed Jesus' sufferings into the victory of life over death ("he [God] heard when I cried to him . . . and I shall live for him," Psalm 22:24, 29).

According to Paul in 1 Corinthians 15, the hope implicit in the resurrection of Jesus means hope for us all. In his long meditation on resurrection, Paul presents the evidence for Jesus' resurrection (15:1–11), takes to task those who say that there is no resurrection (15:12–19), affirms that Christ has indeed been raised (15:20–34), reflects on the nature of the resurrected body (15:35–49), and presents a picture of the remaining eschatological events and the place of the risen ones in them (15:50–58). Because Christ has been raised, our faith and our hope are not in vain. And faith and hope in Christ and his resurrection are strong antidotes to suffering.

Possibilities and Problems

Just as death and resurrection constitute an approach to Jesus' suffering, they represent an approach to our suffering as well. The New Testament places Jesus' suffering and our suffering in the context of the paschal mystery of Jesus' death and resurrection. On one level, suffering is part of human life and so is nothing unusual. But the paschal mystery situates the sufferings of believers in the privileged context of Jesus' death and resurrection. No one has made this point as eloquently as Paul does: "I want to know Christ and the power of his sufferings by becoming like him in his death, if somehow I may attain the resurrection from the dead" (Philippians 3:10–11).

In the context of death and resurrection, it is clear that Jesus' sufferings have great significance. They were the prelude to his own vindication. They made it possible for all people to aspire to and enjoy access to God, justification, sanctification, and salvation. And if Jesus' sufferings have such significance, so may our sufferings have significance for ourselves and for others.

The death and resurrection of Jesus also provide the basis for a theology of hope. As the example of Jesus shows, evil and suffering do not have the last word. As people of faith we look forward to sharing more fully in the glory of the risen Christ. In the present we live with the conviction that Christ has freed us from the dominion of sin and death and for life in the Spirit. In different ways Paul and John affirm that eternal life has already begun through our incorporation into Jesus' death and resurrection. This way of looking at life is confident and hopeful because the source of our confidence and hope is Jesus' death and resurrection.

And yet even here there are some problems. Some object that in this context the sufferings of Jesus are granted too much significance. If (as the Gospels suggest) Jesus was aware of the significance that his sufferings would have and he willingly embraced them, it can seem easier for him to have suffered than it may be for someone like Job, who finds no meaning in his suffering. Others contend that the New Testament writers may be too optimistic about what Christ's death and resurrection actually do for people in the present. Sin, suffering, and death are persistent parts of human existence. Still others observe that the New Testament's concentration on the sufferings of Jesus and their benefits for believers can produce an excessively narrow outlook to the exclusion of other valid humanistic and philosophical approaches to the mystery of suffering.

Questions for Reflection, Discussion, and Prayer

1. Do you find any wisdom in Ben Sira's approach to death?

2. What is the same and what is different in the approaches to death in 2 Maccabees and the Book of Wisdom?

3. What and why did Jesus suffer?

4. In what sense was Jesus' resurrection a vindication?

5. Has your own participation in the paschal mystery ever helped you in dealing with suffering?

Chapter Eight

Suffering for the Gospel

"Yet if any of you suffers as a Christian, do not consider it a disgrace, but glorify God because you bear this name."

—1 Peter 4:16

MOST OF US THINK of the first century of the Christian era as a "golden age." Jesus, the Word made flesh, dwelt among us, giving wise teachings, freeing people from their illnesses and fears, and promising hope for the full coming of God's kingdom. His apostles carried on his mission with remarkable success. The rapid development of the Christian theological vocabulary was truly amazing, and the organizational patterns and church offices that emerged in this period have stood the test of twenty centuries.

However, in admiring the achievements and successes of the first-century church, we can fail to recognize how much suffering was part of the experience of the earliest Christians. In the Greco-Roman world of the first century, the early Christians constituted a tiny minority; they had little or no social status or political influence. They suffered in various ways and dealt with their suffering especially in the light of Jesus' own suffering (and his resurrection).

The documents treated in this chapter—Paul's letters and Acts, Hebrews, 1 Peter, and Revelation—can be regarded as pastoral-theological responses to many problems, but especially to the sufferings that their addressees were enduring. Paul, the great apostle to the Gentiles, labored tirelessly to spread the gospel and to found new churches, and met much physical and spiritual suffering along the way. Those who were Jews by birth, like the Roman Christians addressed in Hebrews, gradually came to recognize the enormity of the theological claims being made about Jesus, and so faced the choice of returning to a more traditional form of Judaism or going a separate way from their kin. As a minority movement, the Gentile Christians of northern Asia Minor addressed in 1 Peter stood apart from their neighbors, and so met opposition because of their "different" beliefs and ways of acting. The refusal of the Christians of western Asia Minor addressed by the Book of Revelation to participate in Roman civil religion because it might compromise their faith in the one God and Jesus as Lord caused at least sporadic persecutions and the threat of more. What binds together these very different writings is their focus on the person of Jesus as an example and as a source of hope in the midst of suffering.

The Sufferings of Paul the Apostle

Of the twenty-seven documents contained in the New Testament, thirteen are attributed to the apostle Paul. And the second half of the Acts of the Apostles is dominated by the figure of Paul. Paul's encounter with the risen Christ transformed someone who had persecuted the followers of Jesus into the most famous proponent of Christian faith. At the core of Paul's theology was belief in the saving significance of Jesus' death and resurrection. He made the early Christian confession about Jesus' death and resurrection for us and for our sins the basis of his pastoral theology, and brought it to his work of spreading the gospel and of founding churches. Paul's identification with Christ was so complete that he could proclaim that "it is no longer I who live, but it is Christ who lives in me" (Galatians 2:20).

Paul's interpretation of Jesus' death as a sacrifice for sins and our participation in it has already been treated on pp. 62–65. Having identified himself so totally with Christ, Paul had to expect that suffering would be part of his own life and especially of his mission as an apostle. In 2 Corinthians 11:24–28, Paul presents a long list of what he endured in spreading the gospel: "Five times I have received from the Jews the forty lashes minus one. Three times I was beaten with rods. Once I received a stoning. Three times I was shipwrecked; for a night and a day I was adrift at sea; on frequent journeys, in danger from rivers, danger from bandits, danger from my own people, danger from Gentiles, danger in the city, danger in the wilderness, danger at sea, danger from false brothers and sisters; in toil and hardship, through many a sleepless night, hungry and thirsty, often without food, cold and naked. And, besides other things, I am under daily pressure because of my anxiety for all the churches."

Paul had founded the largely Gentile Christian church at Corinth in Greece and moved on to continue his apostolic work. As he kept in touch with the Corinthian Christians by emissaries and letters, he learned to his horror that some church members were boasting about their special knowledge and spiritual gifts. In response to this pastoral problem Paul put forward his paradoxical theology of the cross (see 1 Corinthians 1:18–25). The cross, of course, was an instrument of torture and death. And yet the cross of Christ was God's way of restoring right relationship (justification) with humankind. The cross was God's way of rendering foolish the wisdom of the world. While the crucified Jesus appeared to be a stumbling block to Jews and foolishness to Gentiles, for believers like Paul the crucified Jesus is "the power of God and the wisdom of God" (1 Corinthians

1:24). The symbol of the cross redefines wisdom and folly as well as power and weakness. The cross brings about a total reversal of values and serves to place Paul's apostolic sufferings in the context of the sufferings of Jesus.

And so as Paul, in 4:8–13, brings to a climax his response to the spiritual virtuosi at Corinth, he boasts not about his positive achievements but about his personal weaknesses and sufferings for the sake of the gospel. While ironically characterizing the Corinthians as rich and as kings, he describes himself and his coworkers as "a spectacle . . . fools for the sake of Christ . . . weak . . . in disrepute . . . hungry and thirsty . . . poorly clothed and beaten and homeless . . . weary . . . reviled . . . persecuted . . . slandered . . . like the rubbish of the world, the dregs of all things." There is, of course, a rhetorical strategy at work here. By using irony Paul hopes to undercut the pretensions of his opponents and so bring them to their senses. But there is also every reason to assume that Paul believed what he wrote. Once the cross becomes the dominant religious symbol, one begins to view weakness and suffering in a very different light.

The Second Letter to the Corinthians begins and ends with reflections on Paul's sufferings as an apostle. In the opening benediction (1:3–11) Paul blesses God as the one "who consoles us in all our affliction." He interprets his own afflictions in the light of Christ's sufferings ("just as the sufferings of Christ are abundant for us") and as undertaken "for your consolation and salvation."

Large sections of 2 Corinthians are devoted to Paul's defense of his apostleship. As in 1 Corinthians, Paul often celebrates his weakness and suffering as God's instruments for the spread of the gospel: "we have this treasure in clay jars, so that it may be made clear that this extraordinary power belongs to God and does not come from us" (4:7).

Chapters 10–13 in 2 Corinthians constitute a full-scale defense of Paul's apostleship. It appears that other Jewish Christian missionaries had come to Corinth after Paul's departure and questioned his gospel and his credentials as an apostle. Their attack on Paul became quite personal, and Paul quotes some of their criticisms of him: "For they say, 'His letters are weighty and strong, but his bodily presence is weak, and his speech contemptible'" (10:10).

In his "fool's speech," Paul alludes to his positive credentials as an apostle and to his own visionary experiences. But he prefers to dwell on his sufferings (see 11:24–28) and recounts God's answer to his prayer that his "thorn in the flesh" (whatever it was) might be taken from him: "My grace is sufficient for you, for power is made perfect in weakness" (12:9). Again Paul—or rather, the mystery of the cross—has turned everything upside down. And so Paul can proclaim: "Therefore I am content with weaknesses, insults, hardships, persecutions, and calamities for the sake of Christ; for whenever I am weak, then I am strong" (12:10). This powerful expression of Christian freedom explains why Paul could be so fearless in the midst of all his sufferings undertaken for the spread of the gospel.

Paul wrote to the Philippians from prison. In reflecting on his situation as a prisoner in Philippians 1:12–26, Paul rejoices that his suffering had positive results in spreading the gospel. His imprisonment made it possible for his captors ("the whole imperial guard," 1:13) to hear the gospel, and it encouraged other Christians "to speak the word with greater boldness and without fear" (1:14). And so Paul could dismiss as irrelevant the attempts by rival Jewish Christian missionaries to add to his sufferings.

The outcome of his imprisonment was still unclear when Paul wrote to the Philippians. He might be released, or he might be put to death. In either case, Paul regarded the result as something positive. If he were to be put to death, he would be "with Christ" even more fully. If he were to be released, he would be free to carry on his work as an apostle. Since for him "living is Christ and dying is gain" (1:21), Paul could not lose. His only concern was that Christ be exalted and God be glorified. Paul believed that eternal life had already begun for him in baptism, and so he considered physical life and death as of equal value.

Paul is also a major figure in Acts. He recounts his trans-
forming experience of the risen Christ three times (chaps. 9, 22,
26). He undertakes difficult and dangerous journeys all over the
Mediterranean world. He endures opposition from Jews and
Gentiles alike and, when he returns to Jerusalem, he is arrested
and put on trial. When Paul appeals to his status as a Roman cit-
izen, the Roman judge Festus tells him: "You have appealed to
the emperor; to the emperor you will go" (Acts 25:12). The Acts
of the Apostles ends with Paul under house arrest in Rome, still
"proclaiming the kingdom of God and teaching about the Lord
Jesus Christ with all boldness and without hindrance" (28:31).
Despite all obstacles, the Paul of Acts continues the work begun
by Jesus (see Luke 4:16–30) and goes on proclaiming the good
news of salvation.

Suffering as Divine Discipline (Hebrews)

The "letter to the Hebrews" is neither a letter nor to "Hebrews."
Rather, it is best understood as a sermon ("my word of exhortation," 13:22) addressed to Jewish Christians who were becoming discouraged in their new faith. Its author was not Paul, as its
language and content show. Who exactly the author was, however, is not clear. The early church writer Origen concluded
that only God knows who wrote Hebrews. Likewise, the date
and place of its composition are not clear, although Rome in the
sixties of the first century A.D. is an attractive proposal. In this
scenario the author would be encouraging Jewish Christians at
Rome to remain firm in their Christian faith despite their alienation from the local Jewish community and the threat of persecution from the Roman government.

The author of Hebrews was an effective preacher, inter-
weaving expositions of biblical texts and exhortations to hold
firm in Christian faith. The biblical expositions show that
Christ is the key to and fulfillment of the Old Testament Scriptures. To go back to Judaism would be a mistake. He urges his

readers not to "drift away" and thus "neglect so great a salvation" (2:1, 3).

The central theological message of Hebrews is that Jesus Christ is both the perfect sacrifice for sins and the great high priest who willingly offered himself for sins. The work as a whole is a rich theological interpretation of the saving significance of Jesus' death and resurrection. It sets the suffering of Jesus in the context of the biblical concept of vicarious (for others) and expiatory (for our sins) sacrifice. The contribution of Hebrews to a sacrificial understanding of suffering has already been treated on pp. 65–66.

There is also an apocalyptic or eschatological dimension to the problem of suffering in Hebrews. As the author brings his sermon to a close, he quotes Haggai 2:6: "Yet once more I will shake not only the earth but also heaven" (12:26). To those who remain faithful and act upon the preacher's exhortations, he promises "a kingdom that cannot be shaken" (12:28).

The more distinctive and characteristic approaches to suffering in Hebrews concern Jesus as our pioneer or leader in suffering, and suffering as a divine discipline.

In Hebrews 2:10 Jesus is called "the pioneer of their salvation perfect through sufferings." The term translated as "pioneer" (*archegos*) can refer to a founder of a city or nation, the scout for an army troop, or a source of good things. The idea is that in his sufferings Jesus has gone before us as our leader, brought about good things for us, and is the origin of lasting institutions (heavenly ones, as opposed to the earthly "shadow of the good things to come," see 10:1).

According to Hebrews, Jesus leads us in the work of salvation. By his going before us and by his bringing about right relationship with God, we now have access to God and can enjoy, at least by way of anticipation, the benefits of salvation. The truly surprising part of Jesus' leadership is the claim that God made Jesus perfect through suffering. Since people in the first century assumed that gods do not suffer, this was a very surprising claim about Jesus. It is also a surprising idea for us who often imagine that suffering must be a sign of God's disfavor and that God has nothing to do with suffering. But the shocking assertion of Hebrews is that the work of salvation took place in the midst of and because of Jesus' sufferings.

As Jesus' brothers and sisters in faith, we share his special relationship with God as the Father, the first fruits of salvation, and his way of suffering. It is the third point that we want to pass over and avoid because we find it so hard. The word of encouragement that the first readers of Hebrews needed to hear was that they belonged to a community of suffering people and that in suffering Jesus was their pioneer and leader.

Another major theme related to suffering in Hebrews is the idea of suffering as a divine discipline. The theme has deep roots in the Old Testament Wisdom Books. For example, Ben Sira warns his students: "My child, when you come to serve the Lord, prepare yourself for testing" (Sirach 2:1). A willingness to accept discipline is a precondition for making progress in the pursuit of wisdom: "If you are willing, my child, you can be disciplined, and if you apply yourself you will become clever" (Sirach 6:32).

The idea of suffering as a divine discipline is used also by the author of 2 Maccabees as a way of explaining the sufferings of faithful Jews under Antiochus Epiphanes and his collaborators in the second century B.C. He assumes the validity of the law of retribution and the notion that suffering is a punishment for sins. He then claims that while God waits to punish other nations "until they have reached the full measure of their sins" (2 Maccabees 6:14), the present sufferings of Israel are to be interpreted as a sign of God's mercy and care. Their purpose is to prevent Israel's sins from reaching their full measure and so meriting even more catastrophic punishments: "Although he disciplines us with calamities, he does not forsake his own people" (2 Maccabees 6:16).

The exhortation to Christians to persevere in their faith and to regard their sufferings as a divine discipline (Hebrews 12:1–13) takes the leadership of Christ as the starting point:

"looking to Jesus the pioneer and perfecter of our faith, who for the sake of the joy that was set before him endured the cross, disregarding its shame, and has taken his seat at the right hand of the throne of God" (12:2). Using the athletic metaphor of the race, the author points to Jesus as the example of endurance in the midst of suffering and death, and describes his resurrection and exaltation in terms of Psalm 110:1 ("The Lord said to my lord, 'Sit at my right hand . . . '").

The preacher urges his audience to consider what Christ suffered as an incentive "so that you may not grow weary or lose heart" (12:3). He also reminds them that their own sufferings have not yet reached "the point of your shedding blood" (12:4). While martyrdom in the sense of death was the fate of Christ and may eventually be their fate, their present sufferings demand another approach—looking upon their sufferings as a divine discipline.

In 12:5–6 the author takes Proverbs 3:11–12 as the biblical text for his exhortation: "My child, do not regard lightly the discipline of the Lord . . . for the Lord disciplines those whom he loves." Then in 12:7–8 he urges his audience to "endure trials for the sake of discipline" and compares God's actions to those of a loving father. Parents who fail to discipline their children show a lack of love, and so the present sufferings are best understood as a sign of God's loving care.

The comparison between human and divine discipline is developed in 12:9–11. If we respect human parents when they discipline us, how much more should we respect God when God disciplines us (12:9). If human parents discipline us for our own good, how much more grateful should we be when God disciplines us "in order that we may share his holiness" (12:10). While the suffering due to divine discipline in the present may seem painful, it will eventually yield "the peaceful fruit of righteousness to those who have been trained by it" (12:11).

Having explained the present sufferings in terms of divine discipline, the author, in 12:12–13, tells his audience not to be immobilized by suffering but rather to get back on the road of discipleship: "Therefore lift your drooping hands and strengthen your weak knees." His advice is to regard the present sufferings as minor obstacles by which one's faith is tested, and to carry on the positive program of Christian life outlined in Hebrews 12:14–13:19. In his approach to suffering, Christ, the leader made perfect in suffering, provides the example and the rationale for putting up with suffering and even embracing it as God's way of disciplining his children.

Suffering With and For Christ (1 Peter)

There are many similarities between Hebrews and 1 Peter. Both are sermons or exhortations. Both presuppose a situation in which Christians are a minority and are suffering for their new faith. Both call for reflection on Christ and his sufferings as the best response to the situation.

The document known as 1 Peter is an exhortation in the form of a letter from the apostle Peter in Rome (indicated by its code name "Babylon" in 5:13). It is directed to Gentile Christians living in various parts of northern Asia Minor (present-day Turkey). Whether it was composed directly by Peter around A.D. 60 or by someone in the "Peter circle" there between A.D. 70 and 90 is a matter of debate among scholars. The Christians addressed in 1 Peter were Gentiles ("once you were not a people," 2:10). They are said to regard their present life as "the time of your exile" (1:17) and themselves as "aliens and exiles" (2:11). These phrases may refer to their spiritual condition as pilgrims in this world or even (as some scholars contend) to their socio-economic status as migrant workers and/or at least socially marginal persons.

There is little evidence in 1 Peter of an organized persecution of Christians by the Roman government. Rather, the suffering undergone by the Christians addressed in 1 Peter was more likely the result of the new lifestyle that they adopted on their conversion to Christianity. Their former friends "are surprised that you no longer join them in the same excesses of dissipation, and so they blaspheme" (4:4). The new Christians do not behave in the same ways as their neighbors and old friends do, and so they are suffering social alienation and ostracism. In their sufferings Peter urges them to take as their example Christ who "suffered in the flesh" (4:1) and reminds them that those who persecute them now "will have to give an accounting to him who stands ready to judge the living and the dead" (4:5).

In 1 Peter the mystery of suffering is placed in the context of the paschal mystery. So strong is its emphasis on sharing in Jesus' death and resurrection that 1 Peter is sometimes described as a baptismal homily or catechesis. Some scholars even think that most of it was composed to accompany the rite of baptism.

The opening benediction (1:3–12) praises God as the one who has caused Christians to be born anew "through the resurrection of Jesus Christ from the dead" and promises them "an inheritance that is imperishable, undefiled, and unfading" (1:4). It acknowledges the reality of their sufferings in the present but dismisses them as temporary inconveniences ("now for a little while you have had to suffer various trials," 1:6) and interprets them as tests that will prove the genuineness of their faith. And it affirms that the Old Testament prophets were really talking about "the sufferings destined for Christ and the subsequent glory" (1:11).

The opening benediction in 1 Peter provides a framework for Christian life in light of the paschal mystery: Jesus' death and resurrection constitute the starting point and basis; eternal happiness with God is the goal or end; and hope, faith, and love are the means in the present. In this framework the present sufferings appear to be only temporary and serve as opportunities for proving the quality of one's identification with Christ in baptism.

In his first exhortation (1:13–2:3) Peter urges the new Christians to discipline themselves and to pursue holiness in all their conduct. He reminds them that they have been "ransomed" from the futile ways that they inherited from their (pagan) ancestors, and that this transformation was made possible through "the precious blood of Christ, like that of a lamb without defect or blemish" (1:18–19). The term *ransom* means to buy back, to redeem. This way of describing the transformation that the early Christians experienced in their new relationship with God was rooted in the monetary transactions involved in redeeming captives or slaves. The early Christians felt that they had been bought back by Christ from an evil master (Satan) and so freed from their captivity to sin and death.

What made possible their new relationship with God was "the precious blood of Christ." This striking image, which is clearly rooted in the Servant Song in Isaiah 53, evokes Jesus' death on the cross and at the same time refers to the new life made possible for all people through Jesus' giving up his life. In that sense his blood is indeed precious. The proper response to the mystery of redemption in Christ is "to live in reverent fear during the time of your exile" (1:17) and to "grow into salvation" (2:2).

Even though the people addressed in 1 Peter were Gentile Christians, Peter in 2:4–10 does not hesitate to identify them as the people of God in terms taken from the Old Testament Book of Exodus (see 19:6): "you are a chosen race, a royal priesthood, a holy nation, God's own people" (2:9). The Jew, Jesus of Nazareth, made possible their inclusion in the biblical people of God. From being no people and from being strangers and aliens, they had become God's own people. What brought them together was not their ethnic identity or social status. Rather, it was their experience of personal and communal transformation through Jesus' death and resurrection that made them into the people of God. The sign and symbol of their becoming God's people was their baptism. They found a spiritual home in the Christian community and a mission to "proclaim the mighty acts of him who called you out of darkness into his marvelous light" (2:9).

The best way to carry out that mission is by showing good example in the concrete historical situation in which these people found themselves: "Conduct yourselves honorably among the Gentiles so that, though they malign you as evildoers, they may see your honorable deeds and glorify God when he comes to judge" (2:12). Note that "Gentiles" refers to their pagan neighbors, since the Gentile Christians are now part of God's people. As the exhortation in 2:11–3:22 indicates, their good example pertains to their life within the political institutions of the Roman Empire and within their households.

In this context, Peter envisions situations in which Christians will suffer for trying to be faithful to their principles. To slaves who suffer unjustly (2:18–25) he counsels patient endurance and urges confidence since God approves of them. He places before them the good example of the suffering Christ. Christ committed no sin and did nothing wrong. When insulted, he returned no insult. When he suffered, he did not threaten others. In the midst of his suffering Christ put into practice his own principles of loving enemies and nonretaliation for evil. Thus Christ provides a good example for suffering people, especially those who suffer unjustly. Moreover, Christ's suffering had an atoning value. He suffered for us and for our sins: "By his wounds you have been healed" (2:24; see Isaiah 53:5). The passion and death of Jesus made it possible for people to be freed from the power of sin and death and to live in right relationship with God.

The missionary strategy of good example may involve suffering. But as Peter notes, "if you do suffer for doing what is right, you are blessed" (3:14). First Peter 3:15–18 provides an outline of this strategy. It entails knowledge of the Christian faith and a willingness to share it, a gentle and respectful manner toward others, personal integrity, courage in the face of opposition and suffering, and following the example of Christ. The values of Christ were not always the values of the Greco-Roman world and did not always make Christians popular (see 4:1–6). In this context Christians should be willing to suffer for doing good and recall that "Christ also suffered for sins once for all, the righteous for the unrighteous" (3:18). Again the appeal is to the example of the suffering Christ and to the atoning value of his suffering.

In 4:12–19, Peter takes up the theme of suffering for the name of Christ. The new values and ways of acting set the Christians addressed in 1 Peter apart from their neighbors and made them a target for hostility and anger. In addressing this kind of social suffering, Peter urges that Christians give no occasion for their persecution: "let none of you suffer as a murderer, a thief, a criminal, or even as a mischief maker" (4:15). His positive point is that suffering for the name of Christ can be an opportunity to glorify God: "If you are reviled for the name of Christ, you are blessed" (4:14). This kind of suffering may also foster a deeper participation in the paschal mystery: "rejoice insofar as you are sharing Christ's sufferings, so that you may also be glad and shout for joy when his glory is revealed" (4:13).

In his farewell remarks (5:6–11) Peter urges these Christians to continue to resist "your adversary the devil," to recognize that other Christians are undergoing the same kinds of suffering, and to realize that after they "have suffered for a little while" God will "restore, support, strengthen, and establish you" (5:10).

In its treatment of suffering with and for Christ, 1 Peter calls upon many of the biblical approaches to suffering: It is only temporary; it is a test; hold on, until God intervenes decisively; follow the example of Christ; and it is participation in the paschal mystery. Its two most memorable expressions concern the vicarious and expiatory character of Christ's suffering: "ransomed . . . with the precious blood of Christ" (1:18–19) and "by his wounds you have been healed" (2:24).

The Christian Apocalypse (Revelation)

The Book of Revelation is a Christian apocalypse. It uses the language and literary devices found in Daniel and other Jewish apocalypses. It addresses innocent people suffering for their religious convictions. It defends God's power and justice by deferring their full manifestation to some future time known to God. However, Revelation's focus on the risen Jesus makes it a Christian apocalypse. Indeed Revelation is aptly called the book of the risen Christ.

The author identifies himself as "John." He recounts his visionary experiences while a prisoner on the island of Patmos "because of the word of God and the testimony of Jesus" (1:9). The composition of the book is customarily dated to late in the reign of the emperor Domitian (A.D. 95 or 96). The book has elements of an apocalypse, a prophecy, and a letter. The purpose is to encourage Christians in western Asia Minor to persevere in their faith in the face of persecution. To carry out this task, John appeals to the resurrection of Jesus as the basis of hope for the eschatological vindication of the suffering righteous Christians and for the punishment of their enemies.

John's first vision (1:12–20) concerns the risen Jesus. The glorious figure identifies himself as "the first and the last, and the living one. I was dead, and see, I am alive forever and ever; and I have the keys of Death and of Hades" (1:17–18). The risen Jesus uses of himself terms ("the first and the last") usually reserved for God. He refers to his own death and resurrection ("I was dead . . . I am alive forever") and claims to have authority ("the keys") over death. As in other New Testament writings, the resurrection of Jesus is understood to be the inauguration of the coming kingdom of God. For suffering Christians it served as the foundation of their hopes for the future and of patient endurance in their present sufferings.

The letters to the seven churches in Revelation 2–3 provide information about the nature of their sufferings. Some communities are criticized for their spiritual "lukewarmness" and for allowing false teachers to lead them astray. There were also pressures from the local Jewish communities who wanted to protect their own status as an approved religious group. But most serious of all was the expectation on the part of the local Roman officials and the general public that Christians should participate in the civil religion of the Roman Empire. This would involve honoring the emperor as a god and worshiping the goddess Roma as the personification of the empire. Faithful Christians could not do this.

The persecution facing the Christians addressed in Revelation was probably on the local level in western Asia Minor rather than spread throughout the empire. And how far it had already developed is hard to discern. But John viewed it as the great contest about who really is "my Lord and my God." Is it the Roman emperor, or is it the risen Jesus?

That question is answered in John's vision of the heavenly court in Revelation 4–5. The only one found worthy to open the scroll with its seven seals is "a Lamb standing as if it had been slaughtered" (Revelation 5:6). The image takes in both Jesus' death and his resurrection. The "Lamb" image evokes the Servant of the Lord in Isaiah 53, but Christ is now gloriously triumphant in the heavenly court. The Lamb who was slain has ransomed by his blood all kinds of people and made them into "a kingdom and priests serving our God" (5:10). Therefore the members of the heavenly court proclaim: "Worthy is the Lamb that was slaughtered to receive power and wealth and wisdom and might and honor and glory and blessing" (5:12). No earthly emperor deserves such praise.

The opening of the seven seals (6:1–8:1) and the sounding of the seven trumpets (8:2–11:19) describe the disasters and punishments that will come upon the earth because the wicked fail to repent. Underlying these apocalyptic scenarios is the conviction that God will punish the wicked and vindicate the righteous. As in Daniel, God's power and justice are affirmed, but their full manifestation is delayed. While at present it may seem that the wicked are triumphing and the righteous are being defeated, in God's plan and in God's time there will be a dramatic reversal.

The central section of the book (chaps. 12–14) portrays the conflict with the aid of some brilliant imagery. The "woman clothed with the sun" is the people of God under attack by "the great red dragon" (Satan). Even though Satan has been defeated in heaven by Michael, he still has power for a short time to persecute the church on earth. Satan enlists the help of "the beast from the sea" (the Roman emperor) and "the beast from the land" (the local official responsible for promoting the worship of the emperor and Roma and for persecuting the Christians). It is, however, in God's plan to protect and save the faithful witnesses (the 144,000) and to defeat and destroy the "unholy trinity" comprised of Satan, the emperor, and the local official. The seven plagues (chaps. 15–16) echo the ten plagues visited on Egypt in the Book of Exodus and are directed against those "who had the mark of the beast [the emperor] and who worshiped its image" (16:2).

The final chapters feature a sharp contrast between Babylon/Rome (17:1—19:10) and the New Jerusalem (21:9–22:7) that is interrupted by a final series of seven eschatological events (19:11–21:8). The cults of the emperor and Roma are parodied by the figures of the beast and the prostitute. Lest anyone miss the point, we are told: "The woman you saw is the great city that rules over the kings of the earth" (17:18). By comparison, the New Jerusalem is like a bride "clothed with fine linen, bright and pure" (19:8). Between the fall of Babylon/Rome and the establishment of the New Jerusalem are seven end-time events: the appearance of Christ the warrior, his victory in battle, the binding of Satan for a thousand years, the first resurrection for the martyrs, the final defeat of Satan, the last judgment, and the new heaven and the new earth.

The key to understanding the Book of Revelation is the recognition that it concerns the problem of suffering and that it takes up the apocalyptic approach found in Daniel and other Jewish apocalypses. It affirms the omnipotence and justice of God, and explains the present sufferings of the righteous faithful as only temporary and as part of God's larger plan. It differs from the Jewish apocalypses chiefly in the central role attributed to the risen Jesus. His resurrection is the ground of hope for the future and the basis of patient endurance in the present.

The risen Jesus, and not the Roman emperor, is "King of kings and Lord of lords" (Revelation 19:16).

Possibilities and Problems

The New Testament texts treated in this chapter provide an eloquent witness to how early Christians interpreted and endured their sufferings in the light of the paschal mystery. By his total identification with Christ and his conviction that eternal life had already begun for him, Paul could accept all kinds of sufferings as he went about his mission of spreading the gospel and founding new churches. To a wavering and discouraged community, the author of Hebrews pointed to Christ as our pioneer in suffering and to the need for accepting suffering as a divine discipline in walking on the way of discipleship. Likewise, Peter put forward the example of the suffering Christ as a model for Christians experiencing alienation and ostracism from their neighbors. And John in Revelation recounted his vision of the risen Jesus as the slain Lamb reigning in the heavenly court and as the one who really deserves the title "King of kings and Lord of lords." For suffering Christians, belief in the risen Christ was a source of hope and endurance.

All these writings are examples of how early Christians thought about the mystery of suffering and dealt with it in the context of the paschal mystery. The major problem with these approaches to suffering is related to their concrete historical settings. While we can learn much from history, we also know that history never repeats itself. The fact that in the first century Christians constituted such a tiny minority within the Greco-Roman world means that some of the practical advice in these documents does not fit very well in social situations where there is a Christian majority (as in the USA). Indeed some scholars argue that only people in minority situations can really understand the Book of Revelation and some of the other New Testament writings. When taken out of their historical contexts, each of the approaches discussed in this chapter is open to abuses or at least to problems. The following questions seek to highlight some dangers involved in translating these biblical approaches to suffering in the new millennium and to stimulate your thinking about them.

Questions for Reflection, Discussion, and Prayer

1. Does Paul's Christ mysticism render him insensitive to his own sufferings and the very real sufferings of others?

2. How does one know—as the author of Hebrews seems to know—when suffering is a discipline or something else (punishment for sin, an occasion for sacrifice, etc.)?

3. Might the patient attitude toward suffering in 1 Peter encourage passivity in the face of evil or abuse?

4. Might the focus on heaven and the future in Revelation lead to lack of concern for problems in our present experience?

5. What elements in these four approaches to suffering are most helpful in making sense of your own experiences of suffering? Which are least helpful?

Epilogue:
The Memory of Jesus

*"This cup is the new covenant in my
blood. Do this, as often as you drink it,
in remembrance of me."*
— 1 Corinthians 11:25

PAUL AND THE EVANGELISTS tell us that as Jesus approached
his final suffering, he shared a meal with his disciples. At
the Last Supper Jesus identified the bread with his body
and the cup of wine with his blood. He told the disciples to do
this as he had done—in memory of him. Set in the context of
the celebration of the Jewish Passover (the memorial of liberation from slavery, the sacrifice of the paschal Lamb), his words
over the cup evoke many of the great symbols of the Bible: the
cup of suffering, the covenant relationship between God and
his people, blood as a sign of both death and life, and the
immortality that comes through memory. These words and
symbols give a thoroughly biblical interpretation to Jesus' suffering and death.

For Christians, Jesus is the best summary of all the biblical
approaches to suffering. At the hour of his death Jesus recites

the great lament psalm of the righteous sufferer (Psalm 22). In his teaching he both upholds and questions the law of retribution. Like Job, he struggles to accept the suffering that he faces (see Mark 14:32–42). He dies on the cross "for us" and "for our sins," and so fulfills his mission "to give his life as a ransom for many" (Mark 10:45). He warns his disciples to expect suffering, while his miraculous healings are signs of the presence of God's kingdom. He undergoes a martyr's death while bearing witness to his own teaching about love of enemies, concern for marginal people, and trust in God (see Luke 23:32–49). His resurrection is the most decisive event yet in the coming of God's kingdom. As the great high priest he is able to "sympathize with our weaknesses" (Hebrews 4:15) because he has been tested in his own sufferings.

When Christians gather in Jesus' memory, they recall the suffering and death of an innocent man who was misunderstood and treated unjustly, who struggled to accept the sufferings that he foresaw, and who gave his life so patiently that one of his executioners proclaimed, "Truly this man was God's son" (Mark 15:39). The story of Jesus' suffering and death is at the heart of the collective memory of Christians. It is the story of a real historical figure, not a fictional or mythical character. We keep alive the memory of Jesus of Nazareth.

The memory of Jesus can be dangerous. It calls into question many of the easy assumptions about life, happiness, and success that most people hold. It confronts us with the realities of misunderstanding, injustice, and innocent suffering. It reminds us that even the one whom we confess to be the Son of God had to struggle to accept God's will made manifest in the grim realities of the cross. And yet the memory of Jesus also places before us the hope that God can and does bring life out of suffering and death, and reminds us that suffering and death never have the last word in the Bible.

According to Mark 3:14, the essence of being Jesus' disciple is "to be with him." Part of being with Jesus is sharing in his suffering and death. While it may be as painful and difficult for us to "remain here and keep awake" (Mark 14:34) as it was for Jesus' first disciples, it is one important way of keeping alive the memory of Jesus.

For Further Study

∾

BIBLICAL STUDIES

Bauckham, R. *God Crucified. Monotheism and Christology in the New Testament*. Grand Rapids: Eerdmans, 1999.

Beker, J. C. *Suffering and Hope. The Biblical Vision and the Human Predicament*. Grand Rapids: Eerdmans, 1994.

Croy, N. C. *Endurance in Suffering. Hebrews 12:1–13 in its rhetorical, religious, and philosophical context*. Cambridge, UK-New York: Cambridge University Press, 1998.

Gerstenberger, E. and W. Schrage. *Suffering*. Nashville: Abingdon, 1980.

Gutierrez, G. *On Job. God-Talk and the Suffering of the Innocent*. Maryknoll, NY: Orbis, 1987.

Harrington, D. J. *Invitation to the Apocrypha*. Grand Rapids: Eerdmans, 1999.

Longenecker, R. N. (ed.). *Life in the Face of Death. The Resurrection Message of the New Testament*. Grand Rapids: Eerdmans, 1998.

McDermott, J. M. *The Bible on Human Suffering*. Middlegreen, Slough, UK: St. Paul Publications, 1990.

Millazo, G. T. *The Protest and the Silence. Suffering, Death, and Biblical Theology*. Minneapolis: Fortress, 1992.

Simundson, D. J. *Faith Under Fire. Biblical Interpretations of Suffering*. Minneapolis: Augsburg, 1980.

Talbert, C. H. *Learning Through Suffering. The Educational Value of Suffering in the New Testament and Its Milieu*. Collegeville: Liturgical Press, 1991.

THEOLOGICAL AND OTHER STUDIES

Bowker, J. *The Problem of Suffering in the Religions of the World*. Cambridge: Cambridge University Press, 1970.

Chopp, R. S. *The Praxis of Suffering. An Interpretation of Liberation and Political Theologies*. Maryknoll, NY: Orbis, 1987.

Hall, D. J. *God and Human Suffering. An Exercise in the Theology of the Cross*. Minneapolis: Augsburg, 1986.

Hauerwas, S. *Naming the Silences. God, Medicine, and the Problem of Suffering*. Grand Rapids: Eerdmans, 1990.

Hauser, R. J. *Finding God in Troubled Times. The Holy Spirit and Suffering*. New York: Paulist, 1994.

John Paul II, Pope. *The Christian Meaning of Human Suffering (Salvifici Doloris)*. In *Origins* 13, no. 37 (1984).

Johnson, E. E. *She Who Is. The Mystery of God in Feminist Theological*

Discourse. New York: Crossroad, 1992.

Kushner, H. *When Bad Things Happen to Good People.* New York: Schocken, 1981.

McGill, A. C. *Suffering. A Test of Theological Method.* Philadelphia: Westminster, 1982.

Metz, J. B. *Faith in History and Society.* New York: Crossroad, 1980.

Moltmann, J. *The Crucified God. The Cross of Christ as the Foundation and Criticism of Christian Theology.* New York: Harper & Row, 1974.

Richard, L. *What Are They Saying About the Theology of Suffering?* New York: Paulist, 1992.

————. *Christ, the Self-Emptying of God.* New York: Paulist, 1997.

Scarry, E. *The Body in Pain. The Making and Unmaking of the Body.* Oxford: Oxford University Press, 1985.

Soelle, D. *Suffering.* Philadelphia: Fortress, 1975.

Surin, K. *Theology and the Problem of Evil.* Oxford: Blackwell, 1986.

Tilley, T. W. *The Evils of Theodicy.* Washington, D.C.: Georgetown University Press, 1990.

van der Poel, C. *Wholeness and Holiness. A Christian Response to Human Suffering.* Franklin, WI: Sheed & Ward, 1999.

Index